"FIVE MINUTES TO A GREAT NIGHT'S SLEEP!"

ADRENAL EXHAUSTION
AND
CHRONIC FATIGUE
HOW TO STOP THE NIGHTMARE

FRED VAN LIEW

FOREWORD BY KEVIN

3RD
N

Adrenal Exhaustion & Chronic Fatigue
How to Stop the Nightmare!
© 2010 – Third Edition
Copyright – Fred Van Liew

ISBN: 978-0-9824428-3-8

Published By: IHSM Publishing

Requests for permissions should be addressed to:
International Health Services Ministries 1850 N. Greenville Ave Suite 184 Richardson, Texas 75081

DEDICATION

This book is dedicated to God, the source of all healing, and to my Savior Jesus Christ, whose willing sacrifice restored me to my Father, and to the Holy Ghost, whom Jesus sent that I might gain understanding.

A special dedication is for my dear friend, Dr. Karl Parker, who left his body Christmas Day, 2009. I will remember him with great joy, while I will miss him very much.

ACKNOWLEDGEMENTS

Special Thanks go to Dr. Robin Hyman, DC for his vast knowledge and scholarship in the art of healing. His many hours of transcription and collaboration have made this book possible. His friendship has meant even more. Thanks also go to Dr. Karl Parker, DC, who has encouraged me for over twenty years to write a book. It is by his own unyielding example that I have proof we can follow the Truth uncompromisingly and ultimately win. Karl is one of my few true heroes in life, and I count him my very close friend. And special thanks go to Kevin Trudeau, whom I have known since his teen years. Kevin has always pushed the envelope to the very edge, while never forgetting the little guy. He has taught me to be more flexible and adaptive. I am proud of him and of his life's work. He is my youngest hero and he is not finished yet. Kevin defines tough love and true friendship. My appreciation also goes to John Dealey and the members of his Advisory Council for their mentoring and brutal honesty in all things business and personal. Thank you Robin, Karl, Kevin and John, for the unqualified love and support you have all given me. Each of you have consistently offered your time and friendship, expecting little or nothing in return. Finally, my sincerest love and appreciation goes to my cherished wife Kathy. She has to live with me every day, and still loves me. She helps keep order in my life, without which none of this would have happened. She also keeps me humble, but then, that may be the ultimate purpose of all wives!

The following professionals are but a few that have significantly impacted me over the years and consequently the content of this book. They are in no specific order.

Dale Peterson, MD, H. Meredith Berry, MD (deceased), Ed Wagner, DC, Victor Frank, DC, Dr. Paul Yanick, Jr., Pal Kardos, Hungary, who died without knowing the impact his private teaching of harmonics had on me while I studied at the Kodaly Institute in Kecskemet, Hungary in the institute's first graduating class. Peter Erdei, and Dr. Leonard Coldwell and his Instinct Based Medicine System. Also, a special thanks goes also to Thurman Scrivner for his early teachings on healing Scripture. His teaching changed my life profoundly, and will be the basis for my next book on healing Scripture. My time spent at Berwick Boys Foundation still remains as the most influential part of my teen life. The life lessons learned on Dyer Island, Maine and in the Berwick Boys Foundation Headquarters and farm in West Bridgewater, Massachusetts. has influenced me to this day. A special thanks also goes to my mother, Francesca, for her scholarly example. She is perhaps more comforted now, knowing it only took fifty eight years for her son to begin to blossom in his literary pursuits.

So now, as for the publishing of this book, you can blame the people above.

CONTENTS

EFFECTIVE HEALTH SUPPORT

Congratulations on obtaining this book. The information you are about to read is going to answer many questions that may have gone unanswered for far too long. So many people are doing everything they are told regarding nutrition, without seeing lasting results in their health. Fred Van Liew has assembled the pieces very nicely, bringing simplicity back to effective health support. The fact that there is no silver bullet is clear. It is also true that good health does not have to be complicated. Supporting the body's natural intelligence is not a new idea, however Fred gets us closer to doing it right. The benefit of doing it right is restored body communication and a natural healing response.

I have been associated with Fred for nearly thirty years, and have always known I could trust in his integrity. His intelligent desire to seek truth has encouraged some of the most brilliant minds to share very special information with him. He, in turn, has been able to make information understandable and products practical without compromise. I would have to say that his inability to knowingly compromise his integrity is one of his greatest strengths, allowing those who listen to move forward in their lives just by knowing him.

Read, apply and take advantage of his recommended products, as well as the information contained in this book. The goal is fewer drugs and more pain free energy every day, and with this book you will find your body rapidly rewarding your efforts.

—Kevin Trudeau
Author of *"Natural Cures They Don't Want You To Know About"*
Consumer Advocate and host of KT Radio, ktradionetwork. com

WHO IS FRED VAN LIEW?

Fred Van Liew is the world's leading expert in water, air and energy as they relate to your health internally and externally. He has acquired a unique understanding of many natural, non-drug healing methods and maintains continued interaction with the providers of effective health care. This allows him to productively communicate with and support the efforts of these professionals, as well as develop effective solutions to water, air and energy pollution now found in our environments. These solutions support optimal health benefits and response in the body. Now known as the *"Water Doctor,"* Fred has twenty-five years of experience in natural health care.

Why does Fred do it?

Fred's life changed in 1987, when his son was poisoned with fluoride and metals from the local water consumed by his wife during conception and after birth. This infuriated Fred, since he thought he had done his homework and had purchased the best water filter for his home. No one had told Fred what the particular filter he purchased would NOT remove. This lack of knowledge had placed a heavy burden on his son's health.

Fred resolved to find out what every type of filter or filtration method did and did not do. Matching his knowledge of filter performance with what he had learned about body function at the cellular level, he determined what kind of water the body needed as an end result. After not finding a single filter that was able to remove fluoride and all the other health compromising chemicals and dissolved solids in the water, Fred started combining different filters and technologies to obtain pure, oxygen-rich water.

Why is Fred Called "The Water Doctor?"

Fred's dedicated research gave him the knowledge needed to apply various technologies in specific water applications, including home water treatment, agriculture, and the environment. It was his goal to educate healthcare providers and their patients on what types of equipment would best suit individual needs.

Over the years, Fred has designed a variety of systems. Some have saved fish from the ammonia found in chloramines entering tropical fish stores. He built an ozone system for a lobster pound in Maine, as well as chemical-free systems for cooling towers. He has developed, selected and installed a variety of effective swimming pool and spa technologies. He has even developed a milk production enhancement for dairy farms, which has resulted in lowering somatic cell counts and bacterial counts in the bulk tank milk.

Fred has become known as the most reliable source for accurate information and quality, high-performance water and air appliances. His six-month money back guarantee remains the longest in the industry. It has given patients, whose lives are often on the line, and their doctors, the confidence to trust his recommendations.

He has communicated truths in natural health care on his radio broadcasts, "Your Health, Your Choice," for over two decades. His infomercials on showering and bathing have helped educate consumers on the health and beauty benefits of removing chlorine and health-destroying chemicals from showers and baths. Research shows that these chemicals are easily inhaled or absorbed through the skin. Also, his infomercials on home air purification appliances helped revolutionize the industry.

Fred has lectured and taught at many health conventions and seminars, and has the unique ability to make complex health issues simple and understandable. Most notably, the introduction of practical essential energy products with bio-energies has created significant improvements in the environment and in people's health.

The combination of Fred's pure water, essential energy, clean air and fermented harmonically balanced whole food nourishment has changed many people's lives forever. This is Fred's passion and purpose. He wishes the best of health to all that read this book.

Ways to reach Fred?

www.HighEnergyHealing.com

Access Free resources to become well informed and save thousands of dollars and years of frustration. Results of Five Minute Sleep Correction Protocol.

www.LifeXtensionSolutions.com

Access Free resources to become well informed and save thousands of dollars and years of frustration. Results of Five Minute Sleep Correction Protocol.

www.FredVanLiew.com

Fred's views on politics, health and water. Not always politically correct. Fred's speaking and training schedule and recommended links.

www.PWBSeminars.com

Keep updated on Fred's speaking and training schedule, workshops and recommended events. Training schedule for Five Minute Sleep Correction (ERCS) and BSA Basics by Dr. Robin Hyman.

www.BullDozerPack.com

Bulldozer Pack details and purchase for health restoration and maintenance. Addresses the electronic pollution in addition to lack of cellular nourishment in vitamins formulas, without artificial stimulation frequently found in health formulas. A comprehensive first month program fully supporting the body's natural intelligence, and its ability to heal. Addresses every need of the body for efficient cell function and nourishment, as well as cellular and metal detox, and body alkalizing.

Contacts: Fred@ewater.com   www.ewater.com

Primary Resource for all foundational health support in Water, Air, Energy and Nourishment.

HARMONICS ARE THE KEY!

How long have you, or someone you know, suffered with fatigue or outright exhaustion; with constant pain or a body that is slow to heal?—With poor sleep and then fatigue in the morning? And then there are the dark circles under the eyes, and the mounting medical bills and drugs, combined with cabinets and drawers full of "natural" supplements in pill, liquid and powder form. How about your spouse who has been so supportive yet has reached the end of his or her ability to understand why you always feel so rundown?

If this is true of your life or someone you know, then this book is for you, because there is hope and there is a solution. Up until now, you've probably tried to take control and tell your body what to do because it wasn't working. That's why you purchased the pills and books and CDs; so you could finally feel better! Well, that philosophy hasn't been working, has it?

Now, you're going to do something different by letting your body make the decisions. You are going to support your body in every way necessary to achieve uncompromising results. But first you must understand the basics and how to implement them correctly, and then use fine-tuning only if needed. Your body has the intelligence to work miracles if you will simply give it the tools necessary.

This book is about what we often call adrenal exhaustion, and how to stop this nightmare. Some of you may have heard previous discussions on this topic during my lectures and radio broadcasts, yet many people have written to me wanting more detailed information on this subject. This book includes detailed information on what adrenal compromise truly is and the steps needed to create your own personal healing plan. I have also included a question and answer section at the back of this book where you will get very candid answers from me.

What we call adrenal exhaustion has little or nothing to do with compromised adrenal glands. It is actually the cells themselves that are shutting down and failing to open up to a functioning state again. This can be due to excessive and non-stop stimulation from electronic chaos and environmental toxins.

I have worked intensely with water and natural health support for nearly 22 years. This became necessary after my son was poisoned from fluoride, metals and other toxins from the public water supply. I was using the largest carbon block filter I could find based on the written research available and what I was told about different types of water filtration and purification. Believing that information was what nearly cost my son his life. The reason for this poisoning was because the carbon block did not remove fluoride from the water found in the public wells of Grand Prairie Texas. Fortunately, all of the fluoride compromised wells have now been shut down. This shows how research alone is not necessarily going to keep you out of trouble. Sometimes good, old-fashioned common sense is also required.

Now, on the issue of adrenal exhaustion, there are going to be things I write which may be new to some of you. I can assure you that a great deal of false and deceptive information has been released for many years. When I share with you the many challenges we are encountering and start to go into what the solutions are—this should bring to you an enormous amount of hope. Everyone who suffers from the symptoms we attribute to adrenal compromise or communication can again enjoy vibrant health.

Some of the biggest challenges we have are microwaves, chemicals, compromised digestion, poor air, and the toxic non-hydrating water that we are consuming. Of course, the most overwhelming of all the toxins influencing the body is our own negative thoughts. I encourage you to do everything that is within your power to take these poisonous thoughts captive and make sure you feed your mind with good things every day.

The Bible is an excellent start. As Ben Kinchlow has always said, the Bible is not a religious book—it is a book of life. You should do everything you can to stay focused on the positive. Think positive thoughts and be sure that any words passing your lips are also positive. This sounds like an over simplification, however I can assure you that it works. It is also the least costly aspect of health restoration and maintenance.

Dr. Leonard Coldwell has excellent material on this subject that should be explored by all. His book, *"Instinct Based Medicine"* and stress reducing CD's have already changed thousands of lives. He has just published *"The Only Answer To Cancer,"* which revolutionizes how we view disease.

Let me also say up front that no matter what I discuss, I make no attempt to be politically correct. I am a Christian. I would rather pray for you and have you healed by God's promises than sell you bottles of fancy pills or formulas. There is, however, a stewardship of your body that is ultimately your responsibility. We must simply remember that healing always comes from God.

So, what you read in these pages has first gone through my glasses based on my Biblical perspective. Please understand that I give you the right to receive whatever I share through whatever glasses or filters you have chosen for your life. In no way am I trying to force any of my beliefs on you. I simply reserve my right to remain who I am, and I am not going to change or tread on eggshells trying to please everybody. I am simply attempting to get the truth out while I still can enjoy seeing people get well using the body's God given intelligence. That is what this book is about!—"The absolute miracle of listening to and trusting the body's intelligence to always do the right thing."

The following chapters will deal with water, nourishment, air, stress, and emotions. They also touch on the spiritual aspect of healing. Most importantly, they will deal with harmonics.

Harmonics are the key! Never forget this.

What are harmonics? Harmonics are the highest vibrational energies in the environment—within our bodies, and outside our bodies. They contain, and are made up of, frequencies. Some frequencies are harmful to the body because these "chaotic" frequencies are non-supportive and can be destructive. Supportive frequencies can be found at low vibrations; however the ones you are lacking most are in the highest vibrational spectrum. These make your body hum along like a well-tuned orchestra, where every organ is in harmony with every system, and every cell is in harmony with every organ. That is the ultimate goal to maintaining a healthy lifestyle, and like everything in life, there are obstacles to obtaining and maintaining this goal.

Never forget that harmonics are the key! You may have done everything else, in your life, perfectly, however without the harmonics you will never achieve the desired health you seek. You must include consistent harmonic support for the body, or you will be greatly disappointed in your final results.

Water can be the chief carrier of these harmonics, both outside and inside the body. Our thoughts and words can create or destroy these harmonics in an instant. The food we eat can also diminish or increase these harmonics. In light of this, your choice of effective protection from man-made chaos from multiple sources today must be addressed, at least until you have restored natural cellular resistance to chaos.

Yes, you can have natural resistance to chaos; however, it is much like practicing spiritual awareness. It would be nice to have it at all times; though few people devote this kind of effort to first learn and then implement the steps and behavior needed to obtain these results.

You will find the information in the following chapters not only practical but most of all within your capabilities. Great choices bring great results, so choose wisely. This book is your first good choice.

Throughout this book I will occasionally recommend certain products, but since products change all the time, always refer to the recommended websites and individuals found in appendix two. This will provide you with up-to-date product information to implement the principles and practices found throughout this book. Again, the products recommended have been found to be excellent, however they are by no means the only way to achieve your goals.

NUTRITIONAL MYTHS!

There exists much confusion and misunderstanding in today's practice of nutrition and health support. Forty years ago we abandoned God's design regarding the living organisms within our body. Modern nutritional "science" decided to put synthetic vitamins, compounds, and chemicals into our bodies, trying to tell it what to do. By doing this they ignored the ten to twelve thousand compounds that are found in real food. How can we expect our body to function properly when we replace these thousands of natural compounds with fifteen, twenty, or eighty synthetic substitutes? History has proven this does not work.

Think about it; we are constantly hearing about numerous complaints, such as fatigue, headaches, muscle pain, muscle tightness, and poor sleep. There are dark circles under people's eyes and some even have puffy faces. We are seeing more blood pressure and sugar metabolism issues. It has been this way for some time. We live with pain and then more pain. We suffer with slow recovery from illness. We experience poor digestion, weak liver function and prostate challenges. I keep hearing more and more about hormonal imbalances and people getting their "customized hormones."

Please, regardless of what you have been led to believe, I'm telling you God did not give you a defective body. Your body has the ability to keep your hormones balanced. This is a fact. We could continue to address the problems of compromised gallbladder functions, stressed kidney functions or clogged lymphatic systems, but, in short, God *did not* give us defective body parts or faulty systems.

Contrary to what most people believe, adrenal compromise or adrenal exhaustion is not usually an adrenal gland problem.

If the adrenal glands are tested, they are almost always found to be functioning perfectly. Now this may come as a surprise to a number of you who have been told, "Look, your adrenal glands need support and that's why you feel the way you do." The reality is that this myth is usually false. The reasons why adrenal formulas rarely work is because they are trying to support a gland that is not compromised!

The first challenge we have then, when it comes to adrenal exhaustion, is to ask: *How do we support the body?* Frankly, we have been sold an enormous amount of false and misdirected nutritional advice for over forty years. It is unfortunate what we have created for ourselves.

The good news is that the body, being the miracle that it is, can turn around almost any condition rather quickly. I have often repeated that if you are using or trying various healing products or treatments, and you are not getting fairly quick or even immediate results, most likely you are on the wrong path to wellness.

Now, I'm talking about seeing and experiencing results

within days or weeks, never mind months. Please don't buy into the idea of, "I'll just stay with it for another month or two." If you're doing the right things, you should notice a response right away. Sometimes, however, this response may seem to be going in the wrong direction for a short period of time, so don't give up too quickly. Think of the homeopathic model, where at times the symptoms appear to worsen for a short period of time as the body mobilizes its resources against the challenge.

Of course, it's going to take a longer period of time for some chronic or degenerative health challenges to completely turn themselves around. However, it should not take your body long to respond. Your body loves it when you take care of it and give it the resources it needs to function properly. It is very intelligent and responds to good stewardship.

Bad Nutritional Science!

The second challenge we face is forty years of bad nutritional science. Think about this: Why is it that an Eskimo who ate blubber and walrus meat did not have nutritional deficiencies? I also ask the same question about an indigenous rainforest tribe that only ate plants and roots. Why is it that they didn't have vitamin or nutritional deficiencies? The answer is simple.

The blubber and walrus meat the Eskimos were eating were loaded with the minerals from the sea—the sea plants and plankton. The minerals in the foods the indigenous rainforest tribe were eating were plant based. Until recently, these minerals were available in a relatively clean environment, with digestion still working the way God had designed it. Biblical guidelines on what flesh to eat keeps us only once removed from the plant diet that those animals consumed. The digestive system would literally break down and ferment those foods containing plant minerals.

This complex, yet completely natural, process would create hundreds of thousands of new compounds from those foods, regardless of what those foods were. The fermentation occurred whether they were nuts, berries, walrus meat, deer meat, or roots. It didn't matter. These newly created compounds were now available to nourish the living organisms that God put into our bodies.

These living organisms are called commensal cells. There are nine to ten commensal cells for every one body cell. Nobel laureate, Joshua Lederberg described this symbiotic relationship of non-human cells and human cells as a "super-organism." Each one of us has approximately 10 trillion human cells in our body. However, there are about 100 trillion non-human cells in the form of these commensal organisms.[1] It is an astonishing fact that we have 10 times more non-human cells than our own cells in our bodies. More astonishing, however, is that these non-human commensal cells have up to 100 times more genes than our own human cells.[2]

Obviously, God designed our bodies to have these organisms for a reason. These living organisms are found throughout the body. They are even in your jaw, and in your bones. They are everywhere inside you. They *should* get nourished from the functioning digestion of plant-based food and supported by the natural coherent energies that are supposed to be in our environment. Sadly, these energies have pretty much been eliminated from our environment, including our food and water; but we'll get into that in future chapters. Just as sadly, our digestion is also severely compromised, and fermentation is no longer taking place in our toxic digestive environment.

These living organisms should be supported by the hundreds of thousands of compounds created by fermentation during the digestive process. Using these resources, commensal cells, would normally create vitamins on-demand for the proper support of the cells in our bodies. Again, God was so smart that He gave us nine to ten of these living organisms for each of our own body cells. Each one of these living organisms has about 300,000 genes. They truly are smart. Each of your body's cells only have about 65,000 genes. So which are smarter, the body's cells or these vital commensal organisms?

God knew the commensal cells needed extra genes to

decide which organisms were undesirable. They would need go after these unwanted pathogens and infection, and even the small parasite hatchlings. These commensal cells can handle difficult infections in a porous jaw or in bone tissue, only if they are supported with proper nourishment and coherent energy. Yes, these commensal cells will take care of these infections, if properly supported.

They also orchestrate the amino acids to take care of your body cells and clean up the environment. Like enzymes in a sewage system that is all clogged up, the enzymes and living organisms in our bodies break down the decaying matter and make sure it gets eliminated from the body properly. This is total body care, without government interference!

The third challenge that contributes to our health issues is the collusion of government, the pharmaceutical industry and companies like Monsanto.

Our food supply not only has a depleted nutritional value, but it has been contaminated with a host of pesticides and insecticides. What's even worse is the genetic modification of our food. The American Academy of Environmental Medicine, on May 19, 2009, announced to physicians that they needed to educate their patients, the medical community and the public; warning them to avoid genetically modified foods (think Monsanto), and also warning about the health risks from eating such foods.[3]

Published studies have shown that when female rats are fed GM soy, the majority of their babies died. The death rate in the control group was only ten percent.[4] It has also been shown that our own DNA mutates from GMO corn and corn products, like high fructose corn syrup.[5]

Genetically modified corn and cotton (think Monsanto) has been produced by adding the genes from *bacillus thuringiensis*. This has been done in order to kill any invading pests by splitting open their stomachs. The companies, using this technology, claim its safety based on the fact that organic farmers use a similar Bt bacteria spray on their crops. While this organic spray may be washed off, it too is not totally safe, as published reports have shown.[6] The Bt-toxin produced by the genetically modified plant cannot be washed off and it is thousands of times more concentrated than the spray used by organic farmers. Reported symptoms from the Bt include allergic and flu-like reactions from inhaling the spray, eating the corn or even handling the cotton![7] Is it any wonder that we are a nation starving for real nourishment?

Monsanto and big government agri-business appear to have it out for us, with the result being a weakening of our immune systems. Already, in 2009, there are two bills currently before Congress that deal with outlawing the growing and selling of organic food, unless you pay large fees and conform to draconian paperwork. You say "That's insane!" Well, these bills are so badly written and so lengthy, that the same Congress that would not read the content of an eight hundred billion dollar bill, probably won't read these and they will pass them. In fact, the house has already passed one without reading it. Once these bills go through it will be illegal for you to grow organic food for yourself and you certainly won't be able to sell it. If you buy organic food, you will also be labeled a criminal. It's simply getting insane. If it's alive, such as a probiotic or anything with living energy, and it's coming into our country, the FDA wants to zap it and kill it. They seem to want to destroy anything that can sustain life.

You may be thinking, "Fred, that can't really be happening! It's our food. Why would our government do such a thing?" I have seen this activity going on for so many years that I have to say it is not a conspiracy. It just appears to be an all-out effort on the part of a global government order to weaken our immune system and our resistance to disease. This includes the use of poisons, metals and live viruses found in vaccines.

In my 58 years of life, I have seen a lot and I have observed the fact that someone wants to make us dependent on synthetic or laboratory drugs and chemicals for the continued survival of our bodies. I believe that when they have weakened our immune systems to the point of compromising our abilities to ward off diseases, they are going to release a bird flu, swine flu pandemic or plague (all manmade bio-weapons) of some kind on the people of the world to reduce the population. I believe, by their own written communication, that they will be happy if they lose fifty percent or more of us.[8] Does this sound scary? You bet it does!

It is up to us to maintain our immune systems and to do all we can to keep our children strong. We are not going to get this done with our present "healthcare" system. They can nationalize it. They can even make it universal. What any government program means to you is that you are going to have to use their drugs, and give up your freedom of choice. Why? This is where the control of the money is and that's where the power resides. We have forces to be reckoned with, whether it's the Rockefellers or others. However, we must not be complacent. We must remain diligent and keep our immune systems strong.

Thyroid Issues on the Rise

We are also seeing a rise in thyroid issues. These issues can be caused from a number of reasons, including fluoride, pesticide exposure and radioactivity. But most importantly, in the majority of instances, you should not treat the thyroid if your adrenal communication is not first addressed.

So, if you do have adrenal communication compromise, this needs to be taken care of before you start addressing your thyroid. When effective support is provided, it usually takes ten to twelve months for the thyroid to come back to a solid functioning state of ninety percent or better. Individuals with twenty to thirty percent thyroid function can still respond.

Thyroid function will begin to increase in most people if the adrenal communication is tended to first. There are times when the thyroid may need additional support from supplemental iodine that is compatible with the body.

Total body nourishment from fermented sources and harmonic supportive balance for the entire body has shown superior results in most cases, even without specific iodine support. Chiropractic adjustments have also supported the body's ability to restore thyroid function.[9,10,11,12]

How do you get your adrenal communication up to a supportive level? This is what we are going to discuss in later chapters. It is very exciting when you address the basics.

What's really happening throughout the body is that the cells are shutting down due to constant stimulatory stresses of all kinds. These stressors usually come from our environment, including electronics, cell phones, radio and cell phone towers, military/civilian radar and satellites, food additives, water poisons, energy drinks, most nutritional supplements, negative energies and even our thoughts.

The cells themselves are shutting down into a sympathetic state and simply not opening up again to a parasympathetic state. The cells, in simple terms, are not effectively getting protection or relief, so they do not feel safe and consequently are shutting down. They must be allowed to feel safe if they are to open up to the functioning parasympathetic state again.

New Improved eDot EMR Blocker for Cell Phones and Blue Tooth. This affordable, practical, and effective protection for every family member's cell phone, earpiece or cordless phone can be purchased at www.ewater.com

HARMONIC CELLULAR SUPPORT

The good news is that all cells are adaptive. It has been observed that almost any loss at the cellular level can be restored when the body is given a little help. God's design is simple yet profound. Coherence is found in the Word. Simple, consistent prayer, reading from Scripture and meditation (time spent with God) can provide exceptional coherence. There is, no chaos in the Word. It must be done consistently, and this is unfortunately, not a part of most people's daily lives.

Like body armor, harmonic support from appliances worn on the body or in a pocket, or placed on a cell phone or computer can produce some serious improvement and is, in fact, recommended. Choosing a protective appliance, which is also effective, is not so easy. We are dealing with very subtle, though powerful energies. Think about the healing power of prayer, or the laying on of hands. When using one or more of God's promises to effect healing, you may understand the nature of these subtle, though powerful, energies.

A Christian can pull the blood of Jesus over their body while making a cell phone call. This can provide from five to fifteen minutes of perfect coherent protection around and within the body. The challenge comes during the rest of the day when you are carrying the phone with you. Testing has shown this blood protection remains for five to fifteen minutes only, allowing you to remove yourself from a bad situation with minimal damage. It does not provide an excuse to remain there. Think of the need for body armor during the rest of the day.

So, it is in these subtle yet powerful quantum energy technologies that we are finding ways to access and amplify the natural protective harmonic energies provided by God in our environment. These have been artificially, though significantly, depressed by our man-made electromagnetic environment, from the wiring in our homes, to all the satellites and communication tools in use worldwide. Even our collective negative and fearful thoughts depress coherent protection.

Those appliances that naturally access and amplify whatever left spinning electron coherence God has provided, known or unknown, appear to show the most promise. Our man-made environment of electronic and radio wave chaos has artificially depressed these natural life-supporting energies. These natural harmonics provide the essential support that allows the body cells to restore themselves to an open parasympathetic state of communication within the body. When the polarized nature of lipid (fat) layers around the body cells gets restored, cognitive function and nerve regeneration are immediately improved. Accessing and amplifying these coherent energies at the highest vibrational coherence is the key to providing the body with the support intended by Original Design.

These natural harmonics should be in the water we drink, and the food we eat. However, most modern water treatment plants do not allow the water to flow over rocks and waterfalls. They add fluoride, chlorine, metal flocculants and other poisons to the water, killing its singing nature, as Dr. Carl Baugh of the Creation Evidence Museum in Glen Rose, Texas has conveyed in his lectures and writings.

Dead water, coming out of the tap, can now be brought back

to life. One way is using appliances that contain harmonic accessing and amplifying technology, like essential energy mugs found on ewater.com, or effective prayer. Yes, even a simple prayer:

"Father, bless this water (or food) and raise its energy according to Your Promises, that it might bring life to my body, in Jesus' name." (Christian prayer example)

When one asks this, expecting God to honor it (2 Cor1:20), the very taste and texture of the water or beverage is improved. This is what structure and harmonics provide. Consistent use of an effective energizing non-stimulating appliance as well as effective prayer can also help the cells develop a resistance to the non-stop assault from man-made environmental chaos.

Unfortunately, this is most likely not enough to protect most people. You should consider effective protection on every cell phone being used by a family member. Blue tooth devices can be even more harmful than the cell phones themselves, and need their own protection along with a cell phone protection device. Without protection, many people have already had cancer form behind the ear from the use of these blue tooth devices.

What is it going to take for us to wake up? Why is the medical community not speaking up on this issue? Is the dollar really that much more important than people's lives? Be responsible and place an effective EMR protective device on all blue tooth and cell phone appliances.

Most cell phone protection is only moderately effective at best. Manipulation of testing with wrong intention, sales oriented research and outright fraud are rampant in this industry. One recently tested device actually decreased the body's energy instantly. Choose carefully after you do your homework. You must, however, make a choice.

Full body protection plus protection on each cell phone provides the kind of redundancy needed in todays electronically messed up world. The EP2 Stress Pendant and the eDot cell phone protector from ewater.com or Trinisol™ may provide the best total synergy today. Ewater.com will always have accurate information and recommendations for continued updates on protective technologies, as these do change and improve over time.

You need to get your adrenal function, or, more importantly, the cells to open up. Dr. Carlo, the famed cell phone researcher, communicated with me at length regarding the intensity and effectiveness of the harmonics in the EP2 Stress Pendant and QuantaWater™. 13

Sixty percent of these highest vibrational harmonics are found in QuantaWater™. Ninety-three percent are found in the EP2 Stress Pendant and Perfect Balance™ spray. They are also found in Harmony Drops™. Dr. Carlo's comments clarified why, when sprayed in water or directly into the mouth, these catalysts are the first that truly appear to allow the cells to open up and again become communicative.

EP2 Stress Pendant

With this support, cells feel safe again, because they now have harmonics which are powerful and yet subtle enough to counterbalance the chaos that is constantly assaulting them. It was exciting to hear Dr. Carlo disclosing this information, as this confirmed results that were already observed. Hearing another scientist talk about this so clearly and excitedly confirmed observed results from Digital Infrared Thermal Imaging (D.I.T.I.).

Dr. Carlo stated unofficially that the EP2 Stress Pendant appeared to protect the cells. This is called primary protection. He couldn't make that statement publicly until he had completed clinical studies. There was great excitement when he revealed that these were the first appliances that not only dealt with this primary protection, but also dealt with the secondary support, which is getting the cells to open up to parasympathetic mode again. He further stated that there is a tertiary restoration, which appears to allow the cells to repair even the DNA damage caused by all of this environmental chaos. This bio-energy technology shows the greatest promise as well as results in the field of electromagnetic and EMR protection. More information can be found on www.ewater.com and www.trinisol.com. Dr. Carlo's books, found in the resource section at the end of this book, are an absolute must read.

ENVIRONMENTAL CHAOS & DISRUPTION

Have you ever found your head or ear feeling very warm or even hot after talking on your cell phone? You might have thought that the battery was perhaps heating up your head, but are you aware that your cell phone seeks a signal with microwaves, just like those found in your microwave oven? A hot dog cooks from the inside out when you place it in your microwave oven. Microwaves generate heat very quickly, agitating water, fats and sugars. Your brain is also made up of fats, sugars and water. And, like the hot dog, a cell phone is doing the same to your head, your hand or your hip—even more so when it is in use. Once a hot dog is cooked, can you uncook it? No! Similarly, can you uncook your brain or body cells once your cell phone has cooked them? No!

Cell phones are now a fact of life, for the majority of people in the world, so it's important to note that it is not just *your* own cell phone that poses a hazard. Four billion cell phones are in use today. These cell phones are connected to a base station, which makes our exposure to energy-depleting far-field radio waves unavoidable in the United States.

Dr. George Carlo, chairman of the Science & Public Policy Institute in Washington, DC, was originally hired by the cell phone industry to prove that cell phones posed no health hazard. When his research showed the opposite to be true, the industry quickly placed distance between themselves and Dr. Carlo's work.

Dr. Carlo has consistently used body response and live tissue response as the foundation for his research when testing effective body protection protocols and appliances. Worldwide, governments have ignored his findings and sided with the cell phone industry.

The military applications of microwaves, including spy satellites, are some of the most hazardous to our health. These place us in a virtual microwave oven day and night. This disrupts the governing and conception vessel meridian functions within our bodies.

The irritating effects of microwaves, particularly from billions of cell phones around the world, are contributing to disrupted DNA repair, a natural God-given cellular design function. A genetic change can occur because of this disruption. A multitude of symptomatology from cell phone use and environmental electronic chaos may manifest from free radical damage, systemic dysfunction and inhibited cellular communication.[14]

These all too common symptoms might include poor sleep, decreased resistance to all forms of stress, autistic behavior syndromes, traumatic stress disorders, multiple chemical sensitivities, organic stress syndrome, and electromagnetic sensitivities. ADD and ADHD in children and adults may be exacerbated by the constant exposure to these microwaves. Some of the beginning symptoms may include excessive fatigue, tingling of extremities, and ongoing pain from the shoulders up, including severe headaches. These may also include foggy thinking, lightheadedness, unusual memory loss, poor concentration, sensitivity to noise and light and even heart palpitations may manifest.

Later symptoms include excessive sweating at night, blood in the stool, ringing in the ears, persistent nausea, and extreme irritability with fits of anger, skin rashes, bumps and vision impairment. These symptoms are common, however rarely traced to environmental chaos from cell phones and communication microwaves.

Where is our medical community on this? They obviously haven't a clue. Many still use no protection on their own cell phones, or those used by their young children.

But there is hope. Simple, effective protection from this damage, as well as harmonic support for the body, has been shown to prevent or reverse these symptoms.

Cell phone use began in 1984. Before that however, we introduced FM radio stations. It was a shocker when a medical doctor, Dr. Dale Peterson, pointed out how dangerous FM transmissions can be to the body. The U.S. government knew that when FM radio stations were introduced into a community, melanoma and other forms of cancer increased dramatically. When some FM stations failed, the communities where they were located would experience a corresponding decrease in melanoma cancer.

This was not made public, and even today most people are unaware of the hazard FM radio signals pose to cellular function. The statistics, however, are there. Your government and your health officials have withheld them from you all this time. Today, we have more FM radio stations than ever, and this is causing a nightmare for our cells. In fact, virtually all communication electronics are, in fact, some form of microwave.

Little wonder that our living cells are shutting down and remaining in a protective, non-functioning, sympathetic state. They are unable to open up to a functioning parasympathetic state where they can communicate and serve their natural design function. This is often labeled adrenal disorder, adrenal fatigue or adrenal exhaustion, but in fact, the adrenal glands are almost always functioning perfectly. It is the cells that are shutting down that cannot call them for help!

Dr. Carlo points out that electromagnetic fields are the foundation for natural biological function and survival. They are the keys to communication within and between living organisms. Our own DNA has an innate intelligence that allows cells to protect themselves from harmful frequencies. The cells can positively respond to harmonic or supportive frequencies, if they have the proper support from nourishment and harmonic resources. These exceptionally high vibrational harmonics in the quantum or nanotesla range are essential, and their presence provides security for cellular function and communication. The lack of these protective, high vibrational harmonics leaves the cells vulnerable to the irritation from microwaves originating from radio waves of all types. Perhaps the most harmful are the FM radio waves, spy satellites, cell phone towers, and cell phone calls from around the world, and finally the cell phones or the wireless headsets themselves.

Dr. Carlo has shown how much faster and deeper the microwaves, originating from cell phone use, penetrate into the head of a ten-year-old compared to the same radiation from a cell phone used by an adult. About eighty percent of brain cells are being affected by cell phone use, according to Dr. Carlo. It is for this reason we must consider effective protection for any child using a cell phone an absolute necessity. Adults can make their own choices, however, it makes no sense to leave the body defenseless against a personal cell phone, as well as all those calls being made by others that pass through our body every second. This radiation irritates the cells of our body much like the screeching tires of an automobile. We know something bad is going to follow that sound. The constant irritation to your cells is also bad and will shut them down as well.

Dr. Carlo has continued his research over several years.

EP2 Stress Pendant

For example, he actually purchased the EP2 stress pendant for the body, the Trinisol™ cell phone protector and the Trinisol™ fermented nourishment for testing. As related earlier, we spent an hour and a half on the phone recently discussing his findings.[15] I was amazed with the amount of knowledge Dr. Carlo had in terms of the cells going from the open parasympathetic mode, to shutting down into the sympathetic mode. This protects the cells as if a heavy metal had just gone by with all its free radical activity, forcing the cells to shut down to a sympathetic mode. Once the heavy metal passes and the cells feel safe again, they will open back up to the parasympathetic mode. Unfortunately, when chaotic microwaves from cell phone calls around the world are present, this safe feeling does not happen and the cells remain in a closed sympathetic mode.

Think about this. No matter where you are in the world, you can receive your cell phone calls. This means those microwaves are everywhere instantly. When you get a call on your cell phone, the call is going through your body, and everyone else's. Likewise, everyone else's calls are going through your body. The cells hate these microwaves because microwaves are cellular agitators. Microwaves produce right electron spinning chaos. A simple analogy can be made to explain this chaos. The agitation, to your cells, caused by microwaves is like scratching a blackboard with your fingernails. Picture your cells being aggravated twenty-four hours a day, seven days a week by these cell phone calls from around the world. Now add your own cell phone, regardless whether you place the phone on your hip or ear.

Have you noticed when you use your phone, either your ear or your headset gets warm? It's not the battery from the cell phone that's causing the heat. You are actually cooking your brain from the inside out, just like a microwave oven cooks a hotdog from the inside out! The fats, water and sugars are what microwaves agitate to create heat. So you're cooking your brain from the inside out with your cell phone. Exciting, isn't it!

So you say, "I keep it on my hip and use one of those blue tooth devices." Well, guess what? The blue tooth is seeking the same signal from the microwave; only this signal is stronger than the cell phone. That is why a number of people using blue tooth devices are finding that they are getting cancer right there under the ear. And lest you forget, we have all kinds of important parts down there by our hips. Remember, once a hotdog is cooked, "How do you uncook it?" You can't do it, so you want to stop the cooking. Stop the nightmare!

Others may think they can simply hold their cell phone away from their body. This doesn't work either. You might ask them how long it takes the blood, cooked by the cell phone in their hand, to flow to their heart, and then go to the rest of their body.

Currently we have cell phone towers emitting their microwaves. We have spy satellites, that can read your license plate, which have been ramped up so high since the wars, that they are literally microwaving us twenty four hours a day, seven days a week. These microwaves affect the governing vessel and conception vessel on top of your head. Are yours being affected? To find out, place the first two fingers of your left hand flat on top of your head while allowing someone to muscle test your right arm. If this arm muscle tests weak, you are being negatively affected. If you do not understand or have confidence to do this yourself, I encourage you to find a practitioner comfortable with basic muscle response testing of some kind to demonstrate this effect.

Today, almost everyone is affected or compromised. Our bodies have a very hard time getting communication through to the cells when this occurs. It's as if the communication cords have been severed. You may begin to discern by your symptoms that the cells themselves are not able to communicate with the adrenals. The adrenals are thinking everything is functioning fine, but in reality your cells are shut down and no longer receiving nourishment. They are not able to get rid of their waste and they are not able to call for help. It's as if their tongues have been removed.

Finally, we need to remember that our own negative thoughts can be a depressing factor to the energy function of our cells. It doesn't matter what kind of stress we have, whether it is work related, financial or even family related stress. These negative thoughts will be detrimental to healthy cellular function and communication if the body does not have the support to handle it properly.

All these disruptions and interferences from our environment, both inside and outside our body, must be addressed and corrected if we want proper cellular response and healing to occur.

WHY WATER ISN'T JUST
WATER ANYMORE

First of all, we should start with some words of caution regarding water. The level of pH in water does not necessarily determine the level of pH in the body. You are not really looking for alkaline or oxygen-rich water, although both can be desirable under the right conditions. However, the presence of either does not mean they will be utilized effectively. A small amount of any acid in pure water will register the water as acidic, but the lack of any real substance will fail to acidify the body. This is often the case of slightly acidic reverse osmosis water.

The smartest thing to do is to alkalize your body with proper nourishment, not water. Sure, you can artificially alkalize your body with ionizers and pH drops of all kinds, as well as coral calcium, but some of these alkalizing methods may jam your kidneys and compromise your lymphatic system. In most cases, you may observe that your health continues to decline.

Even if, by using these alkalizing methods, you do feel better for a while, this is not true healing. The purity, energies and structure of water are far more important factors to your health restoration and maintenance, both short term and long term, than the symptomatic relief of much modern nutrition. Many water catalysts and appliances make claims that simply are not true or are partial solutions at best.

A wise man, when asked what type of water purifier or filter to use, answered in this manner: "If you ask Fred Van Liew, he is going to say reverse osmosis is the best way to go. If you ask WaterWise, they are going to say distillation is the only way to go. If you ask MultiPure, they are going to say carbon block technology is the only way to go." He then said, "What they all agree on, however, is that you absolutely do not drink the tap water. Do your homework and then choose. Just do not drink untreated tap water."

That man was my very close friend, Kevin Trudeau. He has practiced what he teaches for many years and is the real deal. I recommend you listen to him often on www.ktaradionetwork.com and read his books. This is an essential recommendation if you want to know what is really going on in health and politics. His advice on water is still true today, and is a good starting point for our discussion.

The following are some common challenges that must be addressed for optimal health.

Flouride

There is a poison commonly added to water that is more toxic than lead and only slightly less toxic than arsenic. That poison is fluoride. Whether in its sodium fluoride form, primarily a by-product of aluminum and metal smelting, or the more commonly used highly acidic hydrofluorosilicic liquid wash that comes down from superphosphate fertilizer factory smokestacks, this poison disrupts all seven collagen proteins in the body. This includes the collagen that develops tooth enamel in young children. Research consistently has shown that fluoride in water forms some of the most rare cancers known.[16]

In addition to being one of the most abundant substances on the planet, it is highly toxic to the body when ingested, unless previously digested by plants.

Fluoride is almost impossible to remove, once added to water, except by distillation or reverse osmosis. Although there are some communities where fluoride is naturally occurring, most communities have fluoride added. Both forms of fluoride are highly toxic to the body. This can often be seen by mottling of the teeth, which will also be manifesting in bones within the body.

Some filter media, like activated alumina, can reduce sodium fluoride by up to fifty percent. This reduction is far less effective with the more commonly used hydrofluorosilicic acid form of fluoride. Bone Char will reduce either form of fluoride, however the operative term is only reduce, and often not significantly. Other substances and metals in water chemistry can dramatically alter the percentage of fluoride removed.

Our drinking water is being used as the disposal system of this exceptionally toxic poison by government and industry to avoid enormous waste disposal costs. All of this is to the detriment of our health and the health of our children.

Vaccines

Not only are the poisons in drinking water compromising our health, nearly forty toxin-loaded vaccinations are now given to our children, creating a health nightmare for their bodies. Vaccine components like mercury, Thimerosal, 2PE, aluminum, live and dead viral components, formaldehyde, and just about any form of filth they can find are placed in these vaccines.[17,18,19,20] And, although they're implicated in the compromise of our immune systems and even produce death, we continue to be subjected to these injections, sprays and oral innoculations.

Adjuvants like squaline have been shown to produce horrible neurological disorders and autoimmune reactions. Its use increases the negative effect of these questionable substances consistently found in unproven and often untested vaccines.

Vaccine manufacturers are exempt from any liability whatsoever. These manufacturers have no incentive to test for adverse effects before administering these vaccines. The first people to take the vaccine are the test subjects. The combination of fluoride and vaccine poisons accumulating and combining like a chemistry set makes you wonder how even this miraculous body can survive—OR IS IT SURVIVING?

Medical Waste

We are now finding medical wastes in our processed drinking water. Chlorine added to our drinking water combines with pesticides, medical wastes, and other chemicals to produce chlorinated by-products (CBP's). Chlorine reacts with organic matter (decaying vegetation) to form THM's or trihalomethanes. All of these are either cancer causing, tumorogenic, or teratogenic, (interfering with the growth of an embryo).[21]

Heavy Metals

There are often heavy metals in our water, the most common being lead. However, cadmium and zinc are also common, as is copper leaching from pipes, and aluminum, especially in wells. Many east Texas wells were found to have high levels of aluminum. Aluminum is very interesting in that it masks all kinds of problems, including preventing the elimination of acid water conditions and iron. Aluminum is also difficult to remove with just a filter. It requires distillation or reverse osmosis.

Arsenic

Arsenic can be problematic in different parts of the country. Two decades ago in Grand Prairie, Texas, babies were being born with unusual health challenges because of the public wells contaminated with heavy metals, including arsenic, and high fluoride. This nearly cost my newly born son his life, even after the water passed through the largest carbon block filter made at the time.

OOPS!

You see, although I did my homework and chose the best filter recommended, I found out too late that I had been lied to by both the written research and by the manufacturers. Filter manufacturers tell you what their filters will do, but they don't tell you what they will not do. We had women in our Grand Prairie church with distended stomachs and hair falling out from what was later believed to be the water from the wells, which thankfully are now all shut down.

Many other babies were also born with health challenges. Like my son, there were many dental challenges in those early developmental months and years. Shortly after my son birth, our friend's child, born just a few miles away, had his teeth turn to powder shortly after they started growing in. These are a few of the horror stories that drove me into water purification and health support full time.

Nitrates

Nitrates are another example of a serious challenge when found in water. A young couple, with small children, was renting a house with a well that contained about 30 ppm nitrates. When they called, they were told how to immediately correct the problem. They were advised not to even bathe in those levels of nitrates. They procrastinated for over a year, and only called when a brain tumor had developed in one of their children. This tragedy could have been prevented had they taken immediate remedial action.

Hard Water

Hard water is another common challenge in many parts of the country. Seven grains is considered hard and those with water less than fifteen grains hardness (about 250 ppm of calcium hardness) should consider alternatives to typical water softening solutions. Water softening uses salts of one type or another that may compromise our health and the environment. Now, many hard water sources can be treated in the home with no salts or chemicals, while actually improving the environment.

I have successfully treated water that was over 180 grains of calcium hardness, and the doctor that owned that well told us in no uncertain terms that "you did not have to be Jesus Christ" to walk on his well water. A simple request to your water company will get you a current comprehensive analysis of your municipal water, which they are now required by law to provide or they face stiff penalties.

Well Water

Well water should be tested yearly. National Testing Labs have remained a consistent and affordable choice. New media and tank designs can now keep hardness in suspension while improving hard water performance without salt or chemical regeneration. Some electromagnetic solutions been shown to have superior results as well. The new harmonic water treatments further enhance water performance and efficiency without salt or chemicals. Sadly, there are times when salt regeneration for very hard water is the only solution and is actually recommended. When this becomes the exception rather than the norm, our environment will be less compromised.

Other poisons and toxins, like dioxin, are not even tested, as they are often found in water and the municipalities simply cannot afford to remove them. Some are exceptionally toxic, with only small amounts able to pose serious health risks.

These are just a few of the many challenges we face, and our source waters keep changing as well. Cities and towns blend waters from different sources to keep testing results within legally acceptable parameters. This means you really don't know what you are going to get from your faucet or your shower from one day to the next.

Did you know that bathing or showering exposes you to more water born toxins and poisons than drinking that same water?

Every day you climb into a hot enclosed shower, you allow the vapors to concentrate as if you were in a gas chamber. The heat from the shower is vaporizing the volatile chemicals commonly found in your water, including chlorine and its by-products. Your skin cells are screaming for help, trying to close your pores, while your energy is being sapped from your body. Some of you even sing while showering! You get out of your shower thinking you are relaxed, while in reality you are exhausted. You end up with dry skin and unruly hair, and none the wiser for it. Your dry, plugged pores now try to open up, screaming for oil. That oil pushes the old grease and dirt to the surface, often causing "zits" and other unsavory appearances.

Rashes, Itching and Water Softeners

Rashes and itching from showering can disappear by simply using an effective shower filter. A whole home filtration system is even better. A water softener is not recommended unless the water is exceptionally hard, usually at least fifteen to twenty grains hardness. Water softeners do not remove chlorine or chemicals, or may do so for only a very short time. They actually can increase your exposure to the health destroying chemicals, increasing the negative effects of these chemicals. Should a water softener be used on a municipal water supply, a carbon based chemical and chlorine removal filter should follow the softener. New alternatives to salt regenerated water softening can be found on www.ewater.com.

Testing?

Testing as it relates to water purification choices can be deceptive. One research experiment took cadmium and added it to softened water and to water that was hard (mostly due to calcium). The rats that drank the soft water with cadmium got hyperactive, while those that drank the hard water with cadmium did not get so hyperactive. Their conclusion was that hard water was better for you than soft water. This is obviously not true. It simply means that *hard* water with cadmium is better for you than soft water with cadmium.

Exercise caution and discernment when reading research data. When my company, Ewater.com, would seek testing for our filters, the lab would always ask what results I would like. They were surprised when I told them "Real results from real testing." You see, they can set up the parameters of a test to make a filter look much better than it is. Slow flow of water or a very small amount of water may allow certain contaminants to be temporarily held back until more water is passed through the filter. Even a carbon filter will show fluoride reduction with this gimmick. This kind of *"research"* soured us on a lot of testing claims. That stated, quality testing can still be an indicator of actual performance.

My own son was poisoned with fluoride, metals and high dissolved solids flowing right through a huge carbon block selected after much research. The fact that the limitations of carbon block technology were not revealed in the research presented to me almost cost my son his life. This set in motion a quest to find out what every type of water filter or filtration technology would do and what they would not do. Carbon block technology can be an effective filter when used appropriately. When water is fluoridated or high in dissolved solids it is absolutely not appropriate.

Dr. Carl Baugh and Coherent Energy

The primary key to all health, as it turns out, is coherent energy. Water is the most effective carrier of supportive coherent energy, and was always intended to be our source for this energy. God designed water to revitalize itself whenever it is allowed to flow naturally. It is amazing that water can even flow slightly uphill. Dr. Carl Baugh, of the Creation Evidence Museum in Glen Rose, Texas, has researched water for 25 years. The Creation Evidence Museum is a fascinating place to visit. He teaches that vortexes form within vortexes when water is allowed to flow. This creates a momentum of its own as the water flows. It also creates temperature changes back and forth. Every change of temperature degree, up or down, creates more energy. These vortexes within vortexes create this temperature change back and forth, generating more and more living energy within the water.

You can see these vortexes when you're standing over a bridge or near the bridge abutments and you see the water swirling. These are vortexes. When water is flowing down a stream around rocks and sticks, it is creating its own energy. It is interacting with far infrared energies from the sun and the earth. These interact with the magnetic energies found around and throughout the earth. They even come up from such stones as granites. The water is also going over little and large waterfalls breaking the earth's magnetic field. The water is interacting with all these different energies, and then it is oxygenating itself, creating more coherent energy.

So powerful is the effect of this coherent energy that we have found it breaks the bonds of the most dastardly man made chemicals, even pesticides. Twenty years ago in laboratory testing, scientist found that many of these bonds would never break down. Concerned scientists told us it might be hundreds of years, if not longer, before these chemicals would break down. Thankfully, we found that when water is allowed to flow freely in nature, it creates energies high enough to break these bonds. Dr. Baugh calls it the "singing nature of water."

Energies in the true nanotesla range provide the more correct term for these high-level coherent nanotesla harmonics. These are considered the highest vibrational frequencies found here on earth or in the universe. We found this exciting news once we discovered that these would break down even the strongest chemical bonds. Nature can and will heal itself, if allowed to go its course.

Is it so farfetched to believe that your body has the same ability to heal itself? Of course not! We do not have to be subservient to a medical system that encourages people to ask doctors (who have little to no training in nutrition) their advice on whether to eat a good diet or take nutritional support for the body to improve health.

Today, with few exceptions, medical doctors are not allowed to encourage the use of nutrition or diet when cancer or other degenerative diseases are present. In the past medical doctors were legally prevented from using anything outside of chemotherapy, radiation, surgery or drugs for cancer. Thankfully, many hospitals and clinics today are including nutritional support and stress therapies in cancer treatment. Some doctors, however, still avoid this approach and should be avoided whenever possible.

When we look to nanoteslar harmonics, also known as zero

point energies, we find technologies which can take dead water coming out of your tap, and bring its harmonics back to life-supporting levels. The water is dead because of the fluorides, the chlorine, and other metals added to remove yet other metals. Flocculants are added to help sequester metals. We sanitize the water so it will not kill you quickly, but instead you die slowly by accumulating these poisons.

Remember, fluoride is more toxic than lead, and only slightly less toxic than arsenic. Absolutely, without question, every test ever done on fluoride has shown it to be a highly toxic poison. Fluoride has been shown to be cancer causing in every research study conducted worldwide. It's responsible for mottling the bones and making them brittle. Yet it is still dumped into our water because industry and governments must dispose of hundreds of thousands of tons—not pounds—of fluoride produced each year. We are sacrificed because of their need to eliminate the fluoride in an affordable way. It would cost billions of dollars to dispose of it by current regulations. So it is not just an issue of poisoning us, but doing it in a way they can get away with.

You *must* get the fluoride out of the water you are drinking. I know I've said this time and again, but it nearly cost my son his life. I had done my homework. I did my research. I had the largest carbon block filter made at the time. We moved to Texas, from a non-fluoridated city up in Massachusetts that had soft surface water but no fluoride (Unfortunately Worcester, Massachusetts is now fluoridated). We moved to a city in Texas that had seven wells, yet they were all so contaminated with heavy metals and with fluoride at 2.8 ppm that these contaminates were flowing right through the carbon block I had selected. This filter was taking out the chlorine and chemicals, but not the fluoride, nor the dissolved solids or all heavy metals. This nearly killed my son when he was born.

It was 6 months before we knew what had happened and what was going on. His health and life was touch and go for those months. Once we understood it was the fluoride and some of these other poisons that created his health problems, we were able to rapidly turn him around. In the beginning, shortly after his birth, we didn't know if he would even wake up each morning. So many of these challenges were preventable, which is why I am now so opposed to fluoridation.

I can tell you that, energetically, the water coming out of your tap today is consistently in a negative energy range. It doesn't bring energy to your body, which is one of the God designed purposes of water. Rather, it now strips your body of energy, because it is below the neutral energy point. I use a quantum energy measurement scale called the Bovis scale. 6,500 biophoton activating energy units, or Bovis Units, would be neutral to the body. Most tap water averages about 3,800 Bovis. Most bottled water averages 3,200 – 4,000 Bovis. Based on these numbers, every time you drink a bottle of water you are stripping your body of life supporting energy? You need the water, so please drink the water. Simply energize, structure and harmonize your water, when possible, before you drink it.

Dr. Mu Shik Jhon recommends in his excellent book, *The Water Puzzle and The Hexagonal Key* that you take antioxidants or foods rich in antioxidants, because of the lack of structure and low energy of our water, even after it is purified. The body uses these antioxidants, according to Dr. Mu Shik Jhon, to hexagonally structure water. This makes water acceptable and accessible to the cells, maximizing hydration. Ideally, you must structure and harmonize your water before you drink it, or make sure you are rich in antioxidants for effective hydration and utilization.

Let me stress again what I said about synthetic nutrition. You do not want synthetic antioxidants! But rather, you want antioxidant rich foods that will give your body the resources to turn the water that is energetically dead and structurally nonexistent, into hexagonally structured water. This gives the water some life, and allows it to actually hydrate inside the cells, which is where hydration must occur. Water cannot do this if it is not hexagonally structured. When you add harmonic energies to the water, hydration is exponentially increased. I can tell you from extensive testing, over a long period of time, that the water coming out of your tap, even after it's filtered or purified, is not harmonically active. It is not supportive to your body and it's not effectively hydrating your body.

Water is the key. It is the least costly component of your health support. Do not neglect to keep your body hydrated properly and consistently.

Left: This Reverse Osmosis Appliance uses a proven combination of the most effective water treatment technologies known. It provides the water quality you and your family deserve; water that fits your health-conscious lifestyle.

Right: The Vitalizer Plus, with eCrystals hexagonal water appliance now super oxygenates, micro clusters, mineralizes (slightly alkaline), and energizes any pure water in minutes! Therapeutic higher energy water can be obtained in less than an hour.

SENSIBLE WATER SOLUTIONS

Water is not just water. So many different waters can often be found within fifty miles geographically around you, that it quickly becomes apparent that, unlike food nourishment, water is different. It dissolves anything it flows through, creating a random blend of chance minerals and metals that are non-nutritive and are not easily utilized by our body cells. Accepting this fact silences those who promote filthy tap water or even most filtered tap water as being optimal for health support or restoration.

Revitalizing, energizing and harmonizing your water must be considered to maximize the unique and essential role water plays in any health protocol. Consistently consuming enough purified water is the primary reason any protocol succeeds. A lack of consistent hydration leads to failure, regardless of chosen protocol.

The first step is to purify or at least filter your water. Imprints, or memories of poisons, remain in water even after purification. These should be erased to avoid any negative reaction to this imprinted information.

My own son reacted to the memory of fluoride remaining in purified water, even years after his initial exposure during conception and birth. You could see his complexion turn sallow and his eye sockets become sunken, just from the memory imprint of fluoride. Initially we erased these memories using a homeopathic water catalyst and a fractionally distilled aloe vera juice.

Today we find success using harmonic catalysts like QuantaWater™, Perfect Balance™, Harmony Drops™, or appliances like the Vitalizer Plus™ with a Harmonic eCrystal added, and energy mugs similar to those found on ewater.com.

Now, we will look at the most common filter or purifier choices available today. This can be confusing unless you look at what each water appliance removes or fails to remove. Remember always that purified water is simply pure water. It contains oxygen and energy when it falls from the sky, if we ignore man's pollution. Anything else in the water is picked up by chance as water dissolves whatever it flows through, which is entirely by chance.

First Steps in Producing Drinking Water

The removal of iron, manganese or hydrogen sulfide is required before any of the following filters or purifiers should be considered. Staining on appliances or a rotten egg smell would indicate their presence. All wells should be tested before any treatment of the well water is attempted. National Testing Labs has remained the most affordable and consistently reliable lab in North America for many years.

1. REVERSE OSMOSIS

Topping the list would be a quality reverse osmosis system. Reverse osmosis will retain many of the desirable properties of any water entering the system, including energies and structure. Unfortunately, these desirable qualities are absent in the water entering most homes, while many undesirable poisons and imprints remain.

Reverse osmosis systems combine the best elements of sediment, carbon, carbon block and membrane purification. Regardless of any changes to the source water entering the reverse osmosis system, it offers the most effective removal of fluoride, chemicals, metals, dead dirt minerals and organisms potentially harmful to the body.

This is the technology acknowledged to be most effective in removing medical waste such as drugs, eliminated with body waste, which have been discovered present in many tap waters today. All water consumed should be treated with revitalizing and harmonizing technologies or catalysts that erase negative memory imprints.

2. DISTILLATION

The second best method for producing drinking water is distillation. Distilled water is dead water. It is void of energy and oxygen. It is aggressively trying to fill the voids between its water molecules. The esteemed Dr. M.T. Morter details this in his highly referenced textbook, *Correlative Urinalysis*. Distilled water does remove any dead dirt metallic minerals from the water, and when combined with a carbon filter before and after the distillation, will remove volatile chemicals.

The uniquely aggressive nature of distilled water separates it from the much less aggressive reverse osmosis water in that it potentially leaches electrolytes and their energy from the body. Cells will not give up their plant-based minerals, however the lack of the conductive electrolyte minerals is undesirable. Revitalization and harmonic balancing of distilled water eliminates this aggressive nature. Distilled water is often recommended during a cellular detoxification protocol.

3. FLUORIDE REDUCING FILTER PITCHER

Next, a Fluoride Reducing Filter pitcher using an effective media that actually reduces fluoride by up to sixty-five percent can be an economical choice. This is a non-reverse osmosis or distillation process. It is the only filter, at this time, which reduces all forms of fluoride substantially. It also effectively tests for a very high reduction of heavy metals, chlorine, pesticides, bacteria and parasites. This is not to be confused with mixed bed deionization filter pitchers that result in a very aggressive water. More information is available on ewater.com

4. CARBON BLOCK

Carbon Block filters may be found with or without lead removal capability. Carbon Blocks are compressed activated carbon filters that offer exceptional removal of virtually all chemicals, hydrocarbons, chlorine and their combined by-products. They will not remove fluoride, sulfates, nitrates, arsenic, aluminum, phosphates, salts, detergents, metallic and dead dirt minerals, some medical wastes or viruses. Care must be exercised in their use. They are most common and effective as polishing filters for trace chemical removal at the end of reverse osmosis, and under sink technology.

5. KDF/ACTIVATED CARBON

KDF/Activated Carbon combination filters. These have the same limitations as carbon block technology, however KDF®, a Zinc/Copper composite sometimes referred to as redox media, increases the life of the activated carbon while reducing lead and copper levels if they are present. It also adds bacteriostatic properties to any filter, minimizing biological proliferation. KDF-55® turns chorine to a chloride, thus extending the life of activated carbon to more effectively remove hydrocarbons and the more health destroying chlorine by-products. It can also minimize scale and biological build up in filters and membranes. KDF-85® is used when iron and hydrogen sulfide is present.

6. GRANULAR ACTIVATED CARBON

Granular Activated Carbon should not be used alone for most drinking water purposes. It allows too many contaminants and biological organisms to pass through any filter of this type. This includes fluoride, salts, undesirable minerals and metals, medical wastes, bacteria and virus. These filters can actually be a breeding ground for organisms within a filter.

7. BONE CHAR

Bone Char has been used in some drinking water filters. It is charcoal made from cow bones, the best being cow bones from India and fired in Scotland. It is able to reduce fluoride, and is best used in combination with other whole home system technologies for bathing, showering or brushing teeth. It is no longer recommended for drinking water on a regular basis, as it is otherwise similar to an activated carbon filter and its limitations.

8. SPECIALTY FILTERS

Specialty filters for lead removal, arsenic, fluoride, etc. may be added when necessary, however use of an effective reverse osmosis filter system eliminates the need for these add on filters. Fluoride reducing filters are usually minimally effective in reducing fluoride.

9. DEIONIZING MIXED BED FILTERS

De-ionizing mixed bed cartridges make water very pure, however it becomes far too aggressive for use in the body and therefore is not recommended for drinking water purposes.

10. OZONE

Ozone is for biological purification purposes only, with the added ability to moderately break down some chemicals. Ozone is not recommended for ongoing drinking water consumption in most applications and can leave an undesirable taste to the water.

In Review

Adding multiple filters can get a little awkward and should be avoided. It is more sensible to use a reverse osmosis system with a quality thin film composite membrane combined with sediment, carbon and carbon block technology. This will effectively remove almost all water impurities and organisms, known and unknown. Technology that addresses the imprinting and need for revitalizing the water must also be considered. These must be dealt with separately, as previously noted.

Revitalizing, Structuring and Harmonically Balancing Water

Once you purify your water, you want to then energize, structure and harmonically revitalize your water. This provides optimal support of cellular function and communication. When done properly, this will erase the negative memory in water. You must hexagonally structure the water while you increase or replace the life supporting natural harmonic energies that water is supposed to inherently contain, but has lost.

Start with distilled or reverse osmosis technology. Both may be energetically dead, however the distilled water is absolutely dead and is very low in oxygen. The reverse osmosis water is going to retain whatever energies came in from the source tap water. If you start with high energy water, the reverse osmosis product is going to have high energy as well. Unfortunately, nearly all tap water is now in a negative energy state.

It has been written that reverse osmosis strips the life energy out of water. Reverse osmosis does not do this. The remaining energy is going to be the same on the product side of the reverse osmosis, give or take a little, than what enters on the source side. If dead water goes in, then it is obviously dead water that is coming out. You have cleaner dead water, but still dead water nonetheless. Clean dead water remains more desirable than dirty dead water. So let's bring life back to this water.

Place your water into an appliance like a Vitalizer Plus™. Both distilled and reverse osmosis water should be revitalized with a Vitalizer Plus™ machine and an eCrystal with Harmonic BioEnergies added. The VitalizerPlus™ replicates nature's original design, and the Harmonic eCrystal brings back the high level harmonics that takes water from a solid sixty-five percent hydration after the water is spun in the Vitalizer Plus™ without the eCrystal. It brings the treated water up to eighty-five to one-hundred percent intra-cellular hydration when the eCrystal Harmonics are added. These appliances can be found on ewater.com.

Much like a blender in appearance, the Vitalizer Plus™ replicates everything nature creates when water is allowed to flow naturally. Vortexes, far infrared, strong magnetics and oxygenation are combined to produce what may be the most naturally desirable water by the body. Highly supportive harmonic energies now provide cells with much needed coherence and energy protection. This is a foundational key to adrenal communication restoration and maintenance.

The Quantum BioEnergy support technology found in an eCrystal or Essential Energy Mug will access and amplify ninety-three percent of the very highest vibrational energies found in our environment. This technology is like a receiver. It does not contain the energies itself. It accesses and amplifies the energies available naturally in the environment, though they are artificially compromised and diminished by man-made interference.

These technologies do not access the chaotic, right electron spinning energies. They amplify and transfer only the coherent bio-energies to your water. This makes the water far more enjoyable to consume. The simplicity of water made in a Vitalizer Plus™ with an eCrystal allows the entire family to drink and enjoy more water with superior hydration and support for cellular coherence. Any liquid can be placed in an Essential Energy Mug or placed next to any ewater or Trinisol™ BioEnergy appliance to obtain similar results.

Good examples of other options to optimize water utilization might include the use of harmonizing water catalysts such as QuantaWater™, Perfect Balance™ or Harmony Drops™ which also increase hydration to over eighty-five percent inside the cells. These provide harmonics that allow your cells to feel safe from the environmental chaos around them.

Acid/Alkaline Ionizers

Acid/alkaline ionizers, if used with reverse osmosis, can provide an abundance of electrons to the body. This can be beneficial. There are some great reports on what may occur when you load the water with these available electrons. They can neutralize free radical activity and this is very good. However, most alkaline/acid ionizers with their carbon-only filtration are not recommended, as they do not remove fluoride, sulfates, nitrates, arsenic, aluminum, dead dirt minerals, salts, phosphates, detergents or medical wastes from the water.

Carbon and carbon block filters allow fluoride and other filth to remain in the product water. These toxic compounds are efficiently carried into your cellular matrix when treated with the electrolysis technology of ionizers, to act as potential time bombs as they accumulate in the body over time. It is not the alkaline nature of the water, as much as the hexagonal structuring of the water that makes it very efficient in hydration.

Most people are very dehydrated and simple hydration alone makes them feel much better immediately. Artificial alkalizing of the fluids within the body can make a person feel good, while their health actually deteriorates. Alkalizing with dead minerals found in alkaline water from these carbon filtered ionizing machines is not desirable for any health restoration. Temporary elimination of symptoms may be obtained, however, this would not be considered health restoration.

Recently, some acid/alkaline ionizers have been used successfully with reverse osmosis water. This makes them much more acceptable, though considerably more costly than other effective alternatives, such as a Vitalizer Plus™ reverse osmosis combination. You can put reverse osmosis water under pressure through an ionizer. It still creates alkaline water as well as acid water from the small amount of dissolved solids remaining in reverse osmosis water or re-introduced with a mineral cartridge. This can energize the water to about 320,000 biophoton activating units (Bovis measurements), which is about the same as a 27 minute cycle in a Vitalizer Plus™ appliance. This ionized water does not have the harmonics needed to support optimal cellular communication, however, it can be placed in an energy mug with BioEnergy technolgy from ewater.com with excellent results. The harmonic energies are transferred in less than a minute from the mug to the liquid.

If you already own an ionizer, get a reverse osmosis system and put the reverse osmosis water through your ionizer. Hopefully your machine will work with pure water. Use caution if you are encouraged to spend thousands of dollars on an ionizer alone. Much needed nutritional and energetic support can be obtained with better use of these financial resources, other than just trendy ionized water. Very good machines can be purchased for under $2,000.

The need to start with pure water when choosing a filtration or purification appliance will be reinforced when you consider the following. If your filter only partially cleans the water, is it really better to drink water with a little poison versus a lot of poison? Perhaps, however you should not want any poison entering your body from your water!

Water Catalysts

Water catalysts generally make water more hydrating. They are hardly universal in their health support function, as most only add structure to the water without providing useful energetic or harmonic resources. Electrons, alkalinity, hexagonal structuring and microclustering are all buzzwords commonly in use today. The truth is that most water catalysts have either no energy, negative energy or undesired stimulatory energy. You want none of these in your body.

Claims from one water catalyst have said that it increased electron activity. When tested, the water contained only a three percent electron increase. That may encourage one to question the $40 price tag on an eight ounce bottle. Catalysts like QuantaWater™, Perfect Balance™ and Harmony Drops™, on the other hand, are some of the top water catalysts on the market today. These catalysts offer affordable, very high vibrational harmonic support when small amounts are added to any pure water. They make water nearly perfect in its ability to hydrate inside the cells. However, you must do your homework and make your own choices.

Two ounces of QuantaWater™ added to a gallon of any purified, reverse osmosis or distilled water will bring the hydration from about twenty or thirty percent to over eighty-five to one-hundred percent hydration inside the cells. This will even work with spring water, although be careful, as you may not know what remains in the spring water. The QuantaWater™ energizes and harmonizes the nature of any purified water well into the positive supportive range.

Here is an accepted formula for body hydration. You need to drink a quart of water per day for every fifty pounds of body weight. Very few people are consistently drinking enough pure water. You may be thinking, "I couldn't drink that much water!" Yes you can, if you get it structured, harmonized and energized. QuantaWater™, Harmony Drops™ and Perfect Balance™ will structure the water and you'll not only be able to drink more, you'll enjoy it more as well.

It's amazing how easy it is to hydrate when Perfect Balance™ is sprayed into a glass of water. It's like you don't even

Ewater Revitalizing Shower Filter. Energize, revitalize and pamper your body every time you shower or bathe.

have to swallow. The cells receive that harmonically balanced hexagonally structured water much more efficiently compared to water that is not structured.

The cells cannot effectively utilize water that is not hexagonally structured. A high percentage will simply be eliminated from the body. The body must structure the water if it enters in a non-structured state. This is dependent on an abundance of available antioxidants, and often these are in short supply. This explains why some people are drowning in water and still have cellular dehydration.

Shower Filters

When you use an effective shower filter that takes out more than just the chlorine, you get an instant response from a grateful body. You climb out of your shower refreshed rather than exhausted. You sleep better and you work better. Your hair becomes consistently softer, more manageable and elegant. Your skin loses those large pores around the nose and you get baby soft skin. This is not the case with basic carbon or KDF only shower filters. Look for filters with magnetics and far infrared, like those found on ewater.com.

Whole Home Filtration

Whole home filtration is a solid choice for those who are willing to put their health as a top priority. Water softeners should only be used for exceptionally hard water, and they should be used with a chlorine and chemical removal filter. Water softeners can be very harmful to our environment. Fortunately, there are excellent electronic alternatives today that will work in many applications as a substitute for salt regenerated technology.

Whole home filters may contain:

- **Carbon Only:** May be catalytic, activated, or multiple purpose. These may breed biological activity if no energizing or bacteriostatic technology is present.

- **Carbon and Magnetics:** May provide structure and minimize scaling under ideal conditions.

- **Carbon, Magnetics, Far infrared and Harmonic Technology**: Closest to Nature's original design. Provides revitalization of filtered water and may contain KDF bacteriostatic media that also extends life of carbon beds and removes many heavy metals, particularly lead.

- **Electronic Water Softening:** Great improvement in recent years and now affordable and dependable.

- **Salt Regenerated Water Softening:** These are only recommended when extreme hardness is present. These are much overused in most cities and raise salt levels in recycled water from treatment plants as tons of non-native salt is used for regeneration. Reverse osmosis or distillation is a must if water is consumed or used for cooking after flowing through a water softener. Use a shower filter or a whole home carbon based filter after the softener for bathing and showering.

- **Anti-Scale Media:** A newer addition to water softening or conditioning is scale prevention media. These prevent calcium and minerals from adhering to pipes or appliances, without adding any substance or salt to the water. These can often be used in addition to carbon based chemical removal whole home systems with outstanding results and little or no maintenance for years.

Every whole home filter technology has its strengths and weaknesses, and should be combined with a reverse osmosis system for the drinking and cooking water at the kitchen sink. A Vitalizer Plus™ appliance combines very well with a reverse osmosis system for the ultimate drinking water experience.

Water, for the pipes in the whole home, does not have to be the same quality needed for proper internal function within our bodies. If it were that pure, it would leach copper and lead from the plumbing. We need to have the volatile chemicals, chlorine, and chlorine by-products removed for safer bathing and showering, washing clothes and flushing toilets. Fluoride is not absorbed through the skin and does not easily vaporize in a shower or bath. Salts and dead dirt minerals are not easily absorbed through the skin. These are only a hazard once inside the body on a regular basis. Therefore, only a shower filter or whole home filter is needed for these non ingested applications. Water of much greater purity is needed for internal consumption, particularly free of fluoride and biological pathogens. Noting this, anything less than reverse osmosis or distillation is a compromise, and may actually be a serious health hazard.

Swimming Pools and Spas

Swimming pools and spas can be treated energetically now with great, positive results for the body. Energies similar to those found in the highly effective EP2 Stress Pendant can turn a pool or spa into a dream for health support. Although costly equipment can reduce the use of chlorine and algaecides, there is no such thing as a maintenance-free pool. Concentrate on a healthy pool, not one that is maintenance-free. Use www.ewater.com as a resource for pool and spa remediation. You can inexpensively stop dry skin and dry hair, while turning any pool or spa into a pleasant and energizing experience.

EFFECTIVE CELLULAR NOURISHMENT

Synthetic, isolated, and fractionated nutrition creates a stimulatory stress on your body and on your adrenals. This is often the number one cause of compromised immune systems. This also creates a plateau effect and an eventual "crashing" of your body's cellular communication. What we find missing from most nutrition regimens are the coherent energies needed for your body to survive. These energies are no longer in the foods we eat because they are being irradiated (e-beamed), over-processed, genetically modified and/or microwaved. The energies are being brought down to zero, and the definition of zero energy is death. Gone. Lifeless. How can you bring health to your body with dead, lifeless foods?

The answer is fermented nourishment—predigested, whole food, organic, fermented nourishment. Dr. Paul Yanick, Jr. has developed a process that does not produce molds during or after fermentation, nor is refrigeration required. He is perhaps the world's leading researcher and formulator of uncompromised living nourishment. You will shortly understand how important this is. No synthetic or compromised ingredients should be included in this form of nourishment. Products using this process are non-stimulatory and totally supportive of natural body function and design. There can be no raw ingredients that have been X-rayed. The greatest care in fermentation must be taken, so that no mold forms. Mold is our enemy today. This predigested, fermented nourishment is extremely concentrated and made possible as a result of supercritical CO_2 extraction. This process produces extracts up to a ratio of 800:1. This means that a teaspoon of this concentrate equals over a gallon of the original source.

Nutrient rich ferments like Synbiofood™ or NutriBio-Food™, have hundreds of thousands of compounds created only during fermentation. This fermentation process should be happening in the small intestine during normal digestion of real foods, but no longer does because you're so toxic from the food additives and poisons you are consuming.

The nutrients from concentrated fermented nourishment such as Synbiofood™ allow the body to immediately start to clear mold off your liver. Yes, your liver is coated with mold like a greasy sponge! This explains why, when you try to detox your body, you get horrible detox symptoms. This discomfort is unnecessary. You should not be getting these symptoms if the liver is cleared of mold and the lymphatic system is supported before major body correction is attempted. With ferments like Synbiofood™, even systemic molds begin to disappear. This is because the Synbiofood™ nourishes the living organisms within your body, allowing them to function as designed, clearing the body of undesirable poisons, metals and molds.

God has provided nine to ten living organisms for every one of your body cells. These are often called commensal cells, as described in chapter one. When fermented nourishment is combined with the coherence found in water catalysts containing harmonics in the nanotesla range, such as QuantaWater™, Perfect Balance™ or Harmony Drops™, your body response is enhanced. Perfect Balance™ and Harmony Drops™ also clear stagnant energy from within your body, while supporting cellular communication by accessing nearly ninety-three percent of natural nanotesla harmonics. Hydration is maximized when either is added to any pure water.

Communication between cells and the adrenal glands can reach over eighty-five percent in only six to eight weeks with proper and consistent harmonic support and nourishment. This form of communication is referred to as adrenal function. Today, too many individuals have adrenal function of less than twenty-five percent. Until adrenal function is over eighty-five percent, individuals will rarely respond to even the best diet or treatment. Predigested ferments that bypass compromised digestion, combined with coherent energy support and hydration, consistently provide the quickest road to reversing this impediment to health recovery. Coherent energy remains the key.

Testing has often shown that individuals who take handfuls of nutritional products over a long period of time have the greatest compromise in adrenal function or communication. Conversely, it has often been the individuals who took little or no nutritional support who showed the least adrenal compromise. This is not an indication that the second group was healthy, however it does show they have much less stress on their cellular function. It clearly shows that most modern nutritional supplements are stimulatory and interfere with normal body function, including physiological and psychological, and may add to cellular toxicity.

You will also want to make sure you are making polarized essential fatty acids (EFA's) available to the body. There are a significant percentage of EFA's available in uncompromised food ferments, such as SynBiofood™. This is usually not enough in the first month of a supportive or restorative program. This is best when used for maintenance after optimal health is achieved. This first month of restoration often calls for a "bulldozer" approach. You want to go in there and clear the "boulders" off your road to health with this bulldozer, or complete first month protocol. If you don't clear these obstacles off your highway to health in that first month, you will just keep dancing around them in the following months, year after year, never achieving the health you desire. You must use a bulldozer mentality those first thirty days. You must do it once and you must do it right.

The best philosophy is to safely and totally support your body. The body is capable of turning anything around, and the body is the only one that knows how to do it correctly. It has just been a long time since your body has been given the resources needed to get this job done.

These polarized essential fatty acids are found naturally in plants. When found in this natural state, they are already polarized. No matter what the manufacturing process, it appears this essential polarized nature is lost. When EFA's lose their polarized nature, they no longer can support the polarized phospholipids within cell membranes. This prevents the cells from then utilizing EFA's efficiently. You no longer get the efficient nerve regeneration your body requires. You are not supporting cell-to-cell communication. Dr. Paul Yanick, Jr. has developed a process that allows essential fatty acids to remain polarized. They are called SuperCritical EFA's™. They do not need refrigeration, and they do not go rancid. They are absolutely amazing in their function.

SuperCritical EFA's™ are so concentrated that often as few as three drops per day is all most people require when taken with ferments containing natural polarized EFA's like those found in SynBiofood™. You will often feel the difference within days when this predigested, fermented nourishment is combined with harmonic support, maximum hydration, and SuperCrtical EFA's™.

The next key to a first month "bulldozer" protocol is to find probiotics that do not fight each other. These living organisms must remain uncompromised by X-ray or irradiation. For instance, the organisms found in the probiotic mineral ferment Biotical™ are entirely plant based. There are no soil organisms present and they do not fight each other. That is something most people do not consider when they produce probiotic formulas. The organisms must be allowed to self-perpetuate in an environment that has been turned alkaline by an effective first month bulldozer protocol. This would include fermented nourishment like Synbiofood™, harmonic support from Quanta-Water™ and or Perfect Balance™, and SuperCritical EFA's™. These probiotics work best in a ferment of plant based mineral ligans, the most available form of trace minerals possible. Just one capsule a day for a month of a potent probiotic like Biotical™ can repopulate the barren wasteland most of us call our digestive system.

Biotical™, in its fermented base, contains the hundreds of thousands of compounds only created during fermentation. Scientists explain that each of these compounds is unique, and they have yet to be able to name them all. They nourish and harmonically support the living organisms within the body to such an extent that these organisms are able to fulfill their function, going after pathogens, molds and even small parasite hatchlings. This includes candida overgrowth. These organisms can bring candidiasis under control in as little as three weeks when supported by an effective first month bulldozer protocol. If you have raging candidiasis, you may have to take four to five times the normal daily dose of a probiotic like Biotical™ for four or five days. You then reduce to one per day for the remaining twenty-one to thirty days. You may find your candidiasis completely under control if it is used in conjunction with the other core products described above.

You can alkalize the body within days with an effective first month fermented bulldozer protocol that includes hydration and harmonic support, polarized EFA's and Biotical™ probiotics. This is because the body is no longer producing as many systemic acids. This prevents the body from having the need to rob alkaloid compounds from bones to neutralize these acids. Therefore, you are not losing bone mass and you're not getting osteopenia or osteoarthritis. These symptoms simply go away without you consciously treating them.

It's important that you understand the body creates these problems or symptoms as a consequence of what has been done to it. The body does whatever it needs to do to survive. In principle it must maintain an alkaline state, except in certain instances when it needs to descend briefly into an acid state for therapeutic correction.

This brings up the fact that you do not want to alkalize the body with artificial alkaline water and you do not want to alkalize the body with ground coral calcium in capsules. This will simply jam up the kidneys, congest your lymphatic system, and prevent the body from becoming slightly acidic, if and when it determines this is necessary. This may occur when the body fights an infection or similar condition for a few hours or more. You want to allow the body to do what it is designed to do. That is what your chosen protocol must accomplish. Your bulldozer protocol must fulfill this purpose.

It is necessary to clear stagnant energy out of the body's organ systems and meridian points. You may, for example, find that your gall bladder function is shut down. This could be due to your past use of antibiotics, chemotaxic drugs, or even emotional interference. This could be from a long time ago, and the gall bladder function is still shut down—if doctors haven't yet found a way to cut out the organ. God didn't goof. Keep your gallbladder, but get it turned back on. If you do that nutritionally, it can often take months and thousands of dollars, however it can be done.

A TBM doctor, using Total Body Modification technique, can turn the gallbladder back on in just a couple of minutes with the proper correction. This can also be achieved by Body Specific Analysis Technique. It should continue to function if followed with the proper foundational support discussed in this book. There may be other instances where a technique is required to either turn on an organ or system energetically, or make a structural correction to remove any interference.

One of the most health-compromising conditions is a serious jaw infection. Very few health practitioners can effectively eliminate this type of bone infection. The solution lies within the body itself. There is a whole army of living organisms residing within the porous jawbone, as well as all bones within the body. They are usually undernourished and without coherent energy support if an infection is present.

When your first month protocol is used, including the powerful ferments and probiotics found in Biotical™, these organisms come to life within days. The results can manifest in less than ten days. This occurs not by attacking the infection, but rather by supporting natural body function and its organisms. The body takes care of the infection and results in a stronger immune function. This is health restoration and support at its finest. This may require ten times the minimum daily dose of a component like Biotical™ for a week or more. The cost and time frame is negligible when compared to less effective alternatives.

When you use a bulldozer protocol, the body's organisms or commensal cells will have all the nourishment and coherent support they need to come alive and go after virtually any infection. Remember, however, that ferments included in effective foundational support do not treat infection. They support the living organisms that God designed to defend the body from pathogens. Wow! This is so very cool. It sounds so silly for a fifty-eight-year-old author to say this, but it's true. I never cease to be amazed by the body's consistent response to this kind of coherent support. Coherent energies remain the key.

Stimulatory Energy

Another of our biggest challenges is stimulatory energy found in beverages and foods. Do you need to start your day with your coffee? If you need four to six cups of coffee a day to function, you have a severe adrenal function problem. You are living on stimulatory, synthetic energies and you are headed for a major disaster. Coffee, Red Bull, sodas, and nearly every drink out there now are bragging they have more guarana, more caffeine, more green tea, or more kick than the other guy, yet this over stimulation compromises adrenal communication and adrenal function.

Have I mentioned sugar? We are so addicted to sugar, we can no longer enjoy something if it is not loaded with sugar. We have to get off the sugar. It doesn't mean you can't enjoy a little ice cream now and then. You *should* enjoy your ice cream, just not a lot of ice cream. You will enjoy life a lot more if you simply cut out or reduce the sugars. Remember, everything in moderation.

What about sodas?

Nothing can destroyed our health more than sodas. This next statement may shock you. If you are going to drink a soda, drink Coke Classic®. It is probably the only soda out there that still uses any real herbs, which is why the manufacturer has tried more than once to get rid of it. It would be much cheaper and easier to make if they could use chemicals rather than herbs, as is the practice with most sodas. However, it is best to simply get off the sodas. The sugar, the caffeine, and the chemicals combine to energetically deplete your body, while dehydrating the cells. Drinking an equal amount of pure water is the minimum required to rehydrate the cells after the assault every soda inflicts on your body. This is in addition to the one quart of purified energized water per fifty pounds of body weight recommended daily.

My wife was a six to seven Coke® a day lady for years before I met her. I was smart enough not to tell my fiancé to stop drinking Cokes® before I got her to the altar, but I did ask her to put them in the ewater energy mug for a minute or two before she drank them. She agreed, and in just four days she was down to one Coke® a day. It has been that way ever since, and was accomplished with no withdrawal or headaches whatsoever. It is important to note that both the sugar and caffeine can create massive withdrawal symptoms, such as pain and headaches.

So again, how do we stop this adrenal communication nightmare? How do we stop the nightmare of the cells being shut down; or the cells not being able to communicate and chat with each other? How about your body not being responsive or its failure to respond to the nutrition you have been taking? You may have spent enormous sums of money for years trying to turn your adrenal dysfunction around, only to see continued decline and frustration. This time you are going to succeed with fermented nourishment, proper hydration and coherent energies.

Coherence must be in your nourishment and in the liquids you drink. Water is most important, providing it is hexagonally structured, energized and coherent with the very highest vibrational energies. Nothing turns cellular communication and function on faster than water with sixty to ninety-three percent nanotesla harmonics. The key is to take a truly coherent water catalyst like QuantaWater™ with nanotesla harmonics full strength, sipping one teaspoon every two hours for at least six to eight weeks every day until evening. It is like placing a tuning fork to the head that brings the cell harmonics to their peak design. The harmonics pop up like a cork and then slowly go back down, but never quite as low as they were before the sip. This is a process that can take six to eight weeks to rebuild the energetic muscles to where they can remain resilience with diluted harmonic support and the EP2 Stress Pendant, which has been discussed earlier.

You must also hydrate properly with one quart of purified reverse osmosis or distilled water, brought back to life with QuantaWater™, Perfect Balance™ or Harmony Drops™ per fifty pounds of body weight. These all will structure, energize and harmonize any pure water. They will provide coherent energy support for the cells that have shut down into a sympathetic state of non-function. These coherent energies make the cells feel safe again, allowing them to open back to the parasympathetic functioning and communicating state. This must manifest in over eighty-five percent of cellular function for rapid health restoration to occur. This is good, and it is the key.

The good news is, predigested fermented nourishment bypasses compromised digestion and goes right to the cells, possibly even those that are still shut down. This assumption is entirely from observed consistent positive body response, obtained without stimulation from synthetic nutrition or nutrients isolated from whole food sources.

This truly is the most simple and effective protocol available for restoring cellular communication. It relies entirely on the body's intelligence and supports the body's own self-healing mechanisms for effective and complete health restoration. Superior results can be expected when added to effective structural, emotional and spiritual support.

"Bulldozer" Health Builder

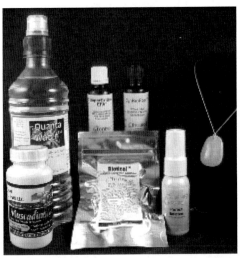

Health Builder Pack, which includes the following complete first month "Bulldozer" support for the body as of Jan. 2010:

- 1 SynBioFood
- 1 Supercritical EFA (lasts approx. 4 months)
- 1 Case (6) QuantaWater
- 1 Perfect Balance
- 1 EP2 Stress Reducing Pendant
- 1 Biotical
- 1 Muscadine Max

ANSWERS TO YOUR QUESTIONS

Q: How do I know what combination of products will work if I'm not sure if it's adrenal exhaustion or adrenal fatigue?

A: When you're supporting your body with the proper energies and food, rather than isolated stimulatory nutrients, your body will know what to do. You don't have to change what you do, whether you have cancer, gout, or migraines. You are going to do the same thing that everyone else does in the first month. There are very few exceptions. However, through testing, you might require a little calcium supplement for a short period of time. You may also need magnesium. Not because you really need it, but because you are weaning yourself off addictions to stimulatory nutrition and diet. Your body might have withdrawal symptoms and may need a buffer at times. That is the only difference.

Otherwise these products allow your body to do what it knows it has to do. You are no longer telling the body what to do. You will no longer take formulas for different diseases because you have tried that for years and it's been frustrating. You are going to do it one more time and you are going to do it right. You are going to go in with a bulldozer and move those boulders off your highway to health. One month only is all it takes. Subsequent months require minimal support to lock in corrections your body can make within that first month.

With proper fermented nourishment, including polarized EFA's, harmonic supportive hydration, effective EMR protective products, and self-perpetuating probiotic ferments with mineral ligands, your body will take care of any disease condition. There will be very few exceptions. There may be times when certain organ systems are shut down due to interference caused primarily by antibiotics, chemo-type drugs, emotional stress or heavy use of synthetic stimulatory nutrition. TBM may be recommended under these circumstances. Look in the *Recommended Resources* section of this book to find a qualified TBM practitioner. TBM can turn your body on by getting its natural biocomputer programs rewired. This allows the body to communicate with itself more effectively.

Q: Can I wear the EP2 Stress Pendant all day?

A: If there is any indication of compromised adrenal function symptoms, start with wearing the EP2 Stress Pendant just two hours per day for two consecutive days, going up just one additional hour every third day. This will re-establish your "energetic" muscle, allowing you to eventually wear the EP2 Stress Pendant all day and even during the night. Wearing the EP2 Stress Pendant beyond your "energetic" muscle may create fatigue, so be aware of your body. Like physical muscle, you must allow periods of energetic rest at the beginning of your journey to re-establish your health. Allow your body to gradually build, and don't push too fast. It could be counterproductive.

Q: So what is the protocol? Do I go to a website?

A: During the actual recommended protocol, you put aside 100% of your synthetic, fractionated or isolated nutritional supplements. This will most likely be all of your current supplements. If your supplements have milligrams or micrograms of individual nutrients on the label they are synthetic. If they are from a whole food and listed in milligrams or micrograms, the body is treating them as synthetic. They're stimulatory, and they're working against you. This is why when you take other stimulatory supplements you get success for a while, plateau, and then you crash. Instead you are going to use whole food fermented nourishment.

You will put aside all of your previous supplements, and give your body three weeks to respond and heal properly. Your new protocol will involve what is referred to as a "Bulldozer" pack. It includes Synbiofood™, Supercritical EFA's™ (which will last 3-4 months. You don't have to reorder those), a pack of Biotical™, QuantaWater™, (6 QuantaWaters™ will last you a month), Perfect Balance™, and an EP2 Stress Pendant. The first month may also include a powerful antioxidant, resveratrol rich, muscadine seed powder such as MuscadineMax™. You can lock in these first month corrections with minimal follow-up nourishment and harmonic support. You will always need some nourishment. The Synbiofood™ and QuantaWater™ for the second and third months are usually all your body requires when added to your Supercritical EFA's™, which lasts four months. When following this protocol you should not experience any type of "healing crisis."

Q: What does all of this cost?
A: This Trinisol™ first month nourishment pack is generally under four hundred dollars. It's recommended you visit www. wellnesslecture.com and use book@wellnesslecture.com as a referring email. This will get you in at no cost to yourself. You will be asked for your name, email and phone number. This is good, as it will allow you to send it to others to get the same information you will hear on "Adrenal Exhaustion 2009 Update" using your email as the referring email. After you've listened to the lecture, it is possible to order the "Bulldozer" pack online for one or two people.

Q: What would the maintenance be after the first month and also after month two and three?

A: During the second and third month it is critical you continue effective harmonic support and hydration. This can be done most effectively with either QuantaWater™, Perfect Balance™ or Harmony Drops™. You would continue using the Synbiofood™, and Super Critical EFA's™. The Biotical™ is only used as needed. Doses of Biotical™ for several days may provide necessary support during the first week of the first month if candidiasis or minor infections are problematic. Your EP2 Stress Pendant will provide constant protection and support as well.

Q: Have you had results with Lymes disease?

A: Lymes disease is primarily a spiritual disease involving a parasite that grabs you. It's pretty well established by most that the parasite carries entities. If you do not deal with it on a spiritual side as well as on the physical side, you are not going to get complete results. When you deal with both simultaneously, and yes, the "Bulldozer" pack will do this, the results will be better than any other Lymes disease formulas available. When you deal with the spiritual side at the same time, you've got nothing to worry about.

Some of these are bold statements, but it comes from successfully working with people, both spiritually and with nourishment. Do it God's way and you will be absolutely overjoyed with the consistency of results. An observational scientist likes consistency of results. If you don't see the same results consistently, why listen to theories? It is all about results.

Q: Are there any additional protocols with Lymes disease?

A: There are some things that should be checked spiritually that may or not be present. If they are, they have to be dealt with. Regarding the protocol discussed, it may require extra Biotical™. You should see the symptoms labeled as

Lymes disease, respond very nicely. Contact the author for recommended spiritual steps.

Q: What about attention deficit and/or mood management challenges? Very often, depending on whom we go to for treatment of an ailment or symptom, we're diagnosed and labeled. However, if you go to an energy practitioner, they may use Applied Kinesiology to determine something different is present.

A: Well again, I like Applied Kinesiology, except it depends on the skill of the practitioner. It can get far too complex. I like TBM a bit more because it relies on the body's intelligence. It lets the body tell you what's going on. There are also techniques for dealing with the emotional components. You can clear them without having to go through "therapy," or knowing what the emotional traumas are.

At the base of most cancers, there is an emotional aspect that has to be addressed and cleared. When you're talking about "focus," ADD/ADHD, manic depression (bipolar) and related symptoms, the EP2 Stress Pendant should definitely be used. The EP2 is very effective at providing the body with resources for coherent energy. It is amazing to observe that many toxic emotions are purged when you drink QuantaWater™. It takes an abundance of coherent energy, for the body to purge toxic emotions. If you don't have the coherent energy the body can't purge them.

People, who have suffered for years with depression, will start drinking the QuantaWater™ while taking the Synbio-food™ and the other recommended products, and find them-selves smiling the next morning, all the while wondering, "Is this supposed to happen?" They'll talk about crying that morn-ing over something they didn't even know what they were cry-ing about. Be assured, they may never cry about it again. They might cry about something else, but whatever the toxic emo-tion was, the body was able to purge it, because it had enough coherent energy to finish the job. It didn't get stuck and go into a depression. Depression is a stuck emotion, where the body doesn't have enough resources to finish the job. An exceptional resource can be found in the works of Dr. Leonard Coldwell. Go to www.instinctbasedmedicine.com.

Q: Wow! That's brilliant. And what does TBM stand for again?
A: Total Body Modification. It's hard sometimes to find a good practitioner. You don't want someone who's had a weekend warrior course. This is where experience can help. Some of you might find it best to fly into Dallas and see a practitioner like Dr. Robin Hyman, DC, who is absolutely brilliant. He has written a number of manuals and textbooks still used in many colleges. He is a brilliant doctor!

Q: What about diabetes?
A: There is nothing that stabilizes blood sugar faster than Synbiofood™. The very first time you take it, you'll see your blood sugar stabilize. It is so natural, so gentle, and yet stabilizes the blood sugar beautifully. TBM also has a great sugar metabolism correction. A person with blood sugar challenges will see their body normalize very quickly when using the Synbiofood™ in the core program. They will see results within weeks or a couple of months, while their dependency on other support will diminish or be eliminated in many cases.

Q: What about the maintenance with diabetes? Clearly they would need to augment their consumption of various foods, such as denatured foods and things of that nature. Perhaps they are using a microwave too much?
A: Let me ask you a question. If a person is going to insist on being really stupid, can anything be done for them? No! There comes a point if a person is going to insist on using microwaved

food, you can't have anything to do with them. Sorry to be so cold, if people haven't got the big picture yet, but I'll say it again. If a microwave will cook a hotdog, it will cook your brain and give you brain cancer. Why are you drinking or eating foods that you put in your microwave? This is not overdramatizing. It is the worst possible thing you could do, other than drink sodas. The maintenance support when diabetes is present is Synbiofood™. It's the same amount, eight drops, twice per day. That's all. Eight drops of Synbiofood™ totally nourishes the body. The food you eat during the day is there to placate your palate and exercise your jaw. You lose your cravings for junk food, which is very helpful. You don't have to preach to people about their diet any longer, unless they're really sick. Just tell them what they should do. If they're going to do it, fine. And if they don't, stop working with them.

Q: Can you tell us a little bit about Type I diabetes?

A: The hardest obstacle to overcome with Type I diabetes is the fact that people have been told to eat so poorly and so inappropriately that it's very difficult for them to change their eating habits. Once they get away from plastic foods and their high protein diet, a type one diabetic will find themselves feeling much better within days. They will be able to travel much easier and will observe many of their symptoms dissipate, if they follow a healthy diet of real food and fermented nourishment with harmonic support and proper hydration.

In fact, a green, live food, diet would be very helpful. If you have any kind of pain, adrenal dysfunction, or if you have health challenges that simply have not responded, you will see them respond, in almost all cases, when you give the body the nourishment it needs. A program on how to only eat greens for a few months is recommended learning. Yes, it may sound like an oversimplification, but you can do it in a way that is absolutely enjoyable. If you eliminated the fruits, juices and sugars from your diet for a few months, you can turn almost any condition around. You will literally see results in days and definitely within weeks. Most people, however, simply will not do it. They would rather die than do it right.

Many people will find their doctor recommending they reduce or eliminate their medication after using effective diet and nourishment. While Type I may take longer, Type II may obtain very desirable results within months.

Q: Regarding the protocol for the Type II Diabetes, you mentioned Synbiofood™. Would they use the Trinisol™ first month "Bulldozer" nourishment pack, or something else?

A: The protocol does not change based on symptoms when the body's intelligence is supported. The symptoms are from the body being out of balance. Think about it. For the body to correct itself, it needs all the resources available at any given time, based on what it decides it needs.

It's like a carpenter going on a job. He brings all of his tools, because he doesn't know what he's going to need. If he only brings half his tools, and realizes he forgot something, such as a drill, he takes a screwdriver and punches an ugly hole, instead of drilling a nice clean hole. We keep forcing our bodies to punch ugly holes.

You should give the body all the resources, properly and energetically, every day. It doesn't matter what your disease is, the body is going to turn it around. You are not nearly as smart as the body. There isn't any group of doctors, no matter who they are, or what their training is, that can even compare to your DNA and the intelligence God has put within every single cell. The body is brilliant.

Our job is to be stewards of our body. Watch the body perform amazing feats that it has not performed when you tried to tell it what to do. We are so programmed to believe we've got to have a certain pill for a certain problem. This is a bad philosophy.

Q: The www.ewater.com site has both the EP2 Stress Pendant and the Cell Phone eDot™. Is there a benefit to doing both? Or, if you just have an EP2 Stress pendant, is that enough protection?

A: The eDot™ can be used on any cell phone or bluetooth device. The Cell Phone eDot™ EMR blocker, is best used on the cell phones themselves. There is an absolute benefit to using both the eDot™ and the EP2 Stress Pendant. If you have to choose one or the other – you should go with the EP2 Stress Pendant. When you use them both together, they overlap the differences of each. You get about a 99% total protection from your own cell phone as well as everything else going on out there in the environment when used together. There isn't anything more effective for the body than this combination.

Q: Does the same protocol apply to an autoimmune disorder or fibromyalgia?

A: Fibromyalgia will usually respond within a week or two, or three weeks on the outside. Plus, by adding TBM treatment, the fibromyalgia may be turned around within days. When you put the two together, it is simply wonderful. If someone needs this done, fly to Dallas and see Dr. Robin C. Hyman, DC. Continue on the Trinisol™ nourishment, while getting your body's "wiring" put back together. Dr. Hyman knows so much more beyond TBM that when you return home the likelihood of your needing much more treatment may be unlikely. You may find someone locally to do other structural maintenance or even some of the emotional techniques needed. The outstanding work of Dr. Leonard Coldwell for stress and emotions is also recommended.

Q: Should I do a doctor consultation first, so that I can get a good baseline, or do I start with the nutritional support first?

A: You're going to start the fermented harmonic nutritional

support no matter what. The body needs to be nourished, that's a given. You eat, no matter what's going on, because you need the nourishment. The sooner you start the Trinisol™ first month's "Bulldozer" pack the sooner you will have desired results. If a health provider is working on you, it would be best to have your body properly nourished. A balanced and nourished body is going to provide a better response and most likely hold that response longer. Why not improve the benefits that you get from any hands on care? If it's just a phone consultation, you're welcome to call me anytime at 800-659-4426 or email me at fred@ewater.com and we can arrange a time.

Q: I have a girlfriend with MS. Can stuff like that be turned around also?

A: Don't buy into any kind of nonsense. MS (multiple sclerosis) is a label put on a myriad of symptoms. What causes those symptoms can be chemical or emotional. We have seen people with MS respond to nourishment alone. But this response is not observed all of the time, because there are different causes of MS symptoms. The chemical, parasite, emotional, structural or the grouping of these problems can often be found with techniques such as TBM. These treatments then allow the body to harmonically correct itself, and the symptoms often disappear. Homeopathy has had some outstanding results.

Q: Do you believe in doing a detox cleanse?

A: There are times when this is very desirable. With Biotical™ and Synbiofood™ you are going to naturally detox the heavy metals and most poisons in a very gentle way, over a period of time. It will turn on your body and body organisms naturally to clean out the accumulated sludge found in your colon. It is similar to putting enzymes into a septic system.

Yes, there are times when a detox or colon cleanse may be helpful, but not a body detox because it often throws the body out of balance. One exception is the very effective and balanced "BePure®" 21 day whole body cleanse designed by Dr. Leonard Coldwell. You're getting a body detox with the Trinisol™ support, faster than any detox I've seen otherwise, although the "BePure®" cleanse is a very compatible cellular detox. This is a very effective combination for those who can afford to do both.

Q: Where are these products manufactured?

A: Some of them are bottled in the Dallas/Ft. Worth area. The ingredients are sourced from all over the world. The total oversight of the core ferments is by Dr. Yanick himself, as well as the QuantaWater® technology. There is simply no compromise in this man, or in me.

Q: So the ingredients are sent to the Dallas area and bottled?

A: In some cases we use a special bottler here in DFW that is only two and a half years old. Their commercial equipment is absolutely state of the art.

Q: Where does the patient education component come in? Is there information that one can obtain to better understand coherent nutritional and energy support.

A: I believe www.wellnesslecture.com contains the most useful, focused, concentrated and accurate information on the web today. You can find all kinds of information on the internet, however you are constantly having to sort through it, wondering if they really know what they're talking about? www.wellnesslecture.com will allow you to have many "aha!" moments when you listen to the adrenal exhaustion lectures first. There is an interview on water with Kevin Trudeau and I that is still appropriate today. You'll find your answers there. Many of my radio broadcasts, which are archived, will also have an abundance of information. And you can always contact me personally. Most people make it harder than it has to be. It simply doesn't have to be hard.

THE FINAL CHAPTER...
WAKING UP!

Recommended Basics For Restoring Cellular Communication, Detoxification and Function.

Absolutely first is to always protect yourself from electronic and electromagnetic radiation. Personal protection is available, area protection is available, and cell phone protection is available. Use them all if possible. See www.ewater.com.

Hydration is always the first and most important part of any health or health restoration program. People compromised in any way need to purify their water with reverse osmosis or distillation, the two most preferred technologies. Bottled water can be used, as well, if processed in either manner. Bottled water is usually dead or in a negative state energetically, and has little or no hexagonal structure. It rarely has any harmonic energy and does not support or hydrate the body efficiently.

Once purified, your water must be structured, energized and harmonized, thus duplicating nature. The ideal way to do this is with a water catalyst such as QuantaWater™, Perfect Balance™ spray, or Harmony Drops™. These are all simple to use and unlike other catalysts, they all provide the harmonics to make the cells feel "safe," allowing these cells to open up once again into a parasympathetic state.

Maintaining hydration with harmonic support can also be done with an appliance called the Vitalizer Plus™, when a Quantum eCrystal™ with its harmonic BioSupport energy is added. With these products, you can obtain maximum intracellular hydration and solid harmonic cellular support, and it is practical for an entire family. This technology offers the supportive energies essential to cellular support and communication not found in other technologies such as acid/alkaline ionizers.

Protecting your cells from ongoing electromagnetic pollution from FM radio signals, satellites, billions of cell phone calls being made, personal cell phones, computers, electrical wires, cell phone towers, flying or traveling, and of course your own negative thoughts is essential. There is simply no better way to do this today than with an EP2 Personal Stress Pendant. It is great for maintaining focus and provides resistance to distractions, helping you stay calm while providing general cellular harmonic support. This technology is the ultimate choice to include with any real cellular restoration program. An eCrystal Salt Lamp, with Essential Harmonic BioSupport Energy, works perfectly for whole home harmony, with the personal protection offered by EP2 Stress Pendant technology.

The next step is to nourish the cells with hundreds of thousands of compounds found in fermented nourishment. However it is hard to find fermented concentrates without mold. Some recommended favorites would be SynBioFood™ or NutriBioFood™. These are able to help clear mold out of the body systemically while clearing mold off the liver as well. This helps prevent any healing crisis.

Nourishing the body with mold free fermented food will quickly lessen the production of acids by the body, lowering candida mold counts and allowing the body to alkalize naturally. This will also minimize the body having to take alkalizing compounds from the bones, stopping bone lose. Blood sugars stabilize naturally, while the living organisms throughout the body and bone are brought back to life, when fermented food is combined with the harmonics of QuantaWater™ or the other recommended water catalysts. In liquid form, the Syn-BioFood™ requires only eight drops twice per day.

Polarized essential fatty acids, as found in nature, are essential for optimal cellular communication restoration and function. The only polarized source in a supercritical concentrate is found in SuperCritical EFA's™ from either Trinisol™ or ewater.com. These are so concentrated, and uncompromised, that just six drops a day is plenty. If used with SynBioFood™, only three drops are used per day. A single small bottle lasts almost four months. Great for brain function, nerve regeneration and function, polarized EFA's are anti-inflammatory as well.

Probiotics, in one form or another, are used by many people today. However, few people understand how X-rays and shipping can compromise these living organisms. FDA policies that want to kill anything that is alive, make it difficult today to find effective probiotics. Most probiotics are burned up once inside the body because of a hostile environment, which is why symptoms return when you stop taking probiotics.

With a product called Biotical™, you will find uncompromised, powerful probiotics, friendly with each other. These are blended with a dense mineral-ligand ferment, including an abundant source of those hundreds of thousands of compounds created during fermentation. Organics help encapsulate metals, poisons and the toxic carcasses of dead organisms, making elimination possible without crisis.

Outstanding results are obtained when Candida issues are present. Four or five Biotical™ capsules for the first four or five days is effective when candida challenges, or minor infections exist. Followed by one capsule per day, a couple of thirty-capsule packets can make a body very happy within twenty-one days or less. Even jaw infections respond well from the support which Biotical™ provides the living organisms found in the porous jawbone. When supported with up to ten capsules per day, these friendly organisms, which are native to the body, can go after serious bone infection successfully within seven to ten days.

We must deal with high initial cellular toxicity. High anti-oxidant, anti-aging formulas can be very stimulatory, which is not good, especially when cellular communication is already compromised. This stimulatory action can be avoided when using resveratrol, a product made entirely from natural muscadine grape seed without isolating components.

Resveratrol is found naturally in the muscadine grape seed at levels up to forty times more concentrated than other grape varieties. MuscadineMax™ is my selected support for this first month component. MuscadineMax™ is a unique source of anti-oxidant, anti-aging compounds with up to 4,200 ORAC tested per the two capsule daily recommended dose, or 1,600 mgs. This is over 130,000 ORAC in a month's supply, one of the highest available in any natural whole food product. This is highly recommended for healthy skin as well.

Using the combined resources recommended above will provide complete nourishment and hydration for the body, with full harmonic support, that can take away cravings for most junk foods. It will bring a rapid change in the pH and harmony of the internal body environment, while providing a complete toolbox for virtually any challenge the body may encounter.

You do not need other supplements during this protocol, and it would be recommended that existing supplements be set aside, for at least the first three weeks, when this recommended support is started. Most supplements will interfere, especially if they have mg or mcg of individual nutrients on the label. Not all, but most supplements will be stimulatory if added to the recommended protocol.

Sometimes a little extra calcium, about three hundred milligrams a day, is enough for many individuals, for one to three months. Dr. Victor Frank, DC has pointed out that you should not stay on the same form of calcium more than four or five weeks at a time. Change from calcium citrate to a calcium lactate after five weeks, for example. Sometimes a little vitamin C for a few days or weeks may be called for, or the often recommended 400 IU of vitamin D during winter months. These are the only acceptable isolates, except for vitamin B6, that will not interfere while the body makes corrections with its own intelligence.

Vitamin B6 is interesting as an isolate. It is synthetic, made from sludge basically. It is also very inexpensive and found in any drug store. Yet, in today's environment, polluted with synthetic hormones and mimicking compounds, B6 provides the body's reproductive system with the tools to metabolize these synthetic hormones effectively. Again, Dr. Victor Frank, DC has emphasized that 300 mg per day of vitamin B6 as an isolate that should be in every woman's daily routine. It cannot be in a formula of B complex. Nearly all B complex formulas are highly stimulatory, as they are all synthetic or isolated. I have to say feedback has consistently been excellent from those who have used B6. Men usually need no more than 100 mg. It is not as essential for the men.

Other than the optional recommended isolated nourishment, the entire first month protocol can be found in what is called a Health Builder Pack from Trinisol™. The first month contains everything needed to fully support the body and move boulders off your highway to health. This is why it is often call a Trinisol™ "Bulldozer" Pack. The second and third month allow the body to lock in the corrections it has made in its own priority and timing. The second and third month require only the fermented nourishment of SynBioFood™, the hydration of QuantaWater™ catalyst or Perfect Balance™ spray, and the SuperCritical EFA's™. This combination makes the maintenance cost per month among the least costly of any program available, yet the resulting support exceeds virtually any other resource available. The Trinisol™ Health Builder Pack can be obtained from many health providers or on www.ewater.com under the Trinisol™ link.

Finally, we must remember that our emotions, and how we handle stress, can override the very best external and internal support we provide to our body. Dr. Leonard Coldwell has outstanding recordings and books that can be used daily to successfully overcome these individual events and emotions stored in our subconscious and deeper. Reading uplifting material daily, such as the Bible, can contribute greatly to cellular harmony and peace.

HERE IS WHAT FRED VAN LIEW FOLLOWS:
Strengthen the immune system naturally.

Maximized Hydration must be maintained, while providing needed harmonic support for cellular communication:

QuantaWater™: 2 oz per gallon of any purified water for hydration daily & 1 tsp. or sip, full strength, every two hours for maximum harmonic support.

Perfect Balance™ or Harmony Drops™: 1 spray or 1-2 drops per glass of water for clearing stagnant energies from organ systems and meridians and will maximize the hydration and structure of any pure water.

Body Nourishment:
SynBioFood™ or NutriBioFood™: 8 drops twice per day, in water or licked off the back of a hand. This fermented food nourishment provides hundreds of thousands of unique compounds to support the body's own defensive army of living organisms.

Cellular Communication, Nerve regeneration, & anti-inflammation:
Polarized Supercritical EFA's™: 3 drops once per day.

Protective Gut Flora (probiotics):
Biotical™: 1 capsule per day on an empty stomach.

Minerals:
Biotical: 1 capsule per day provides mineral ligands in an exceptional concentration while maximizing their availability.

Morter Trace Minerals: 9 drops per day, one per glass of water. These are plant based trace minerals with exceptional and unique energetic coherence.

Additional Anti-Oxidant source:
MuscadineMax™: 4200 ORAC per two capsule daily recommendation. It is rich in resveratrol with all its natural grape seed co-factors. Not an isolate but a whole seed powder.

Pathogen protection:
2000-8000 IU of vitamin D3.

Vaccinations:
Before receiving any vaccination mist or shot, eat a non-stressful diet, low on meat or hard to digest food or combinations. Living food is best, or lightly cooked vegetables.

Just before flu mist:
Any quality essential oil rubbed in the nostrils, such as peppermint. Great when flying as well.

Just before shot:
20,000 IU of vitamin D3 twice per day, continue for 5-6 days after shot.

After a shot or mist:

In addition to the immune building protocol above:

Continue 20,000 IU of vitamin D3 twice per day for at least 5-6 days, followed by 2000-8000 IU for maintenance.

Biotical™ Capsules: 4 per day for six days. Provides organic matter & minerals to encapsulate poisons and metals found in vaccine.
-or-

Morter Trace Minerals: 7-10 drops at one time in 4 oz water, twice per day for four days, depending on body size.

2 oz Angstrom Calcium, wait 3 minutes, follow with 3 oz SilZinCo Angstrom mineral formula (silver, zinc & copper). Repeat second day.

For nutritional support, my children received half doses when under twelve years of age. They received quarter doses when they were younger than five years.

See a competent TBM (Total Body Modification) practitioner who is qualified with the allergy harmonization protocol. Ask if they can harmonize the body to H1N1 vaccine, metals and poisons. This will support the body's ability to purge these substances without further harm.

Recommended practitioners:
Dr. Robin C Hyman, DC, Dallas, Texas 214-420-5555
Dr. Alan Blum, DC San Diego, CA 619-688-2090

REFERENCE NOTES

[1] Ian William, "The things we carry," *Spirituality & Health*, July/August 2009, 56.

[2] William, "The things we carry," 56.

[3] Jeffery M. Smith, "Doctors warn: Avoid genetically modified food," *Well Being Journal*, September/October 2009, 22.

[4] Irina Ermakova, "Genetically modified soy leads to the decrease of weight and high mortality of rat pups of the first generation. Preliminary studies," *Ecosinform*, 1, 2006, 4-9.

[5] Netherwood, et al., "Assessing the survival of transgenic plant DNA in the human gastrointestinal tract," *Nature Biotechnology*, 22, 2004, 2.

[6] Smith, "Doctors warn: Avoid genetically modified food," 23.

[7] Smith, "Doctors warn: Avoid genetically modified food," 23.

[8] Rima Laibow, MD, http://mefeedia.com/entry/azk-vortrag-codex-alimentarius-dr-rimaelaibow/15028922; Internet.

[9] David Walters, *Applied Kinesiology: Synopsis*, (Pueblo: Systems DC, 1988), 506-508.

[10] Robin C. Hyman, *Applied Kinesiology & Subluxation Analysis*, (Dallas: Enchantment Publishing, 2009), 130-131.

[11] Raquel Martin, *Today's Health Alternative*, (Tehachapi: America West Publishers, 1992), 209-210.

[12] Robin C. Hyman, *Table Assisted Adjusting: An Exposition of the Thompson Technique,* (Dallas: Enchantment Publishing, 2003), 64.

[13] George Carlo, telephone interview by author, 25 November 2008.

[14] B. Blake Levitt, *Cell Towers: Wireless Convenience? Or Environmental Hazard?* Proceedings of the "Cell Towers Forum" State of the Science/State of the Law, (Markham: New Century Publishing, 2001), 275-291.

[15] George Carlo, telephone interview by author, 25 November 2008.

[16] John Yiamouyiannis, *Flouride: The Aging Factor,* (Delaware: Health Action Press, 1993), 72-90.

[17] Cynthia Cournoyer, *What About Immunizations? Exposing the Vaccine Philosophy,* (Santa Cruz: Nelson's Books, 1995), 27-31.

[18] Barbara Loe Fisher, *The Consumer's Guide to Childhood Vaccines,* (Vienna: National Vaccine Information Center, 1997), 29-31.

[19] "Hypersensitivity Reactions to Vaccine Components: 2-Phenoxyethanol," available from http://www.medscape.com/viewarticle/5160454; Internet.

[20] "2 PE in Vaccines", available from http://www.fda.gov/downloads/BiologicsBloodVaccines/ApprovedProducts/UCM126652.pdf; Internet.

[21] John Cary Stewart, *Drinking Water Hazards,* (Hiram: Envirographics, 1990), 134-135.

EAT WHAT YOU ARE!

THE LOGICAL APPROACH
TO HEALTH!

—Robin C. Hyman, DC, LCP, FRC

The best dietary recommendation or advice is to simply observe what the human body is made of and "eat what you are!" The human body requires energy to survive, repair, reproduce and communicate. But where should this source of energy come from? Surprisingly… the best source is NOT carbohydrate.

So where's my energy really coming from?

Scientifically and medically speaking it comes from adenosine triphosphate or ATP for short. Guyton's Textbook of Medical Physiology very specifically details the use ATP for the important functions of synthesis of cellular components, muscular contraction, and transport of molecules across cell membranes (ie: cellular communication). It is also responsible for the energy used for glandular secretion and nerve conduction.[1] Basically all functions of life are powered by ATP!

A long term and more balanced rational approach would be to utilize protein (4 calories per gram) and fats (9 calories per gram!) for this purpose.[2] No part of the human body is techni-cally composed of carbohydrate. Next to water, the two most prevalent macronutrients are proteins and fats.

Life is in the Liver!

The liver is the main organ responsible for handling the metabolism of the foods we eat. It performs functions of carbohydrate, fat and protein metabolism to sustain life. Our bodies can break down carbohydrates into the necessary metabolites to produce ATP. However when too much carbohydrate is provided the excess is converted to fats (triglycerides and cholesterol), while a "sugar spike" is experienced. Human bodies have much more efficient mechanisms to produce ATP from proteins and fats called gluconeogenesis.

To quote directly from Guyton's *Textbook of Medical Physiology*[3]

Carbohydrate Metabolism

In carbohydrate metabolism the liver performs the following specific functions (1) storage of glycogen, (2) conversion of galactose and fructose to glucose, (3) gluconeogenesis and (4) formation of many important chemical compounds from the intermediate   products of carbohydrate metabolism. The liver is especially important for maintaining a normal blood glucose concentration.

Fat Metabolism

Some specific functions of the liver in fat metabolism are (1) very high rate of beta oxidation of fatty acids and formation of acetoacetic acid, (2) formation of most of the lipoproteins, (3) synthesis of large quantities of cholesterol and phospholipids, and (4) conversion of large quantities of carbohydrates and proteins from fat.

Protein Metabolism

Even though a large proportion of the processes for carbohydrate and fat metabolism occurs in the liver, the body could probably dispense with many of these functions of the liver and still survive. On the other hand, the body cannot dispense with the services of the liver in protein metabolism for more than a few days without death ensuing.

So fats and proteins are better energy sources than carbohydrates?

Stryers Textbook of Biochemistry specifically states in Chapter 17 on *Fatty Acid Metabolism* that "triacylglycerols are highly concentrated stores of metabolic energy."[4] Chapter 18 on *Amino Acid Degradation and the Urea Cycle* adds that, "amino acids in excess of those needed for the synthesis of proteins and other biomolecules cannot be stored, in contrast with fatty acids and glucose, nor are they excreted. Rather, surplus amino acids are used as metabolic fuel."[5]

Here again the logic is repeated. Protein and fats can be used as an efficient source of metabolic fuel. These macronutrients are much larger in size than the simple six carbon atom molecule composing glucose. Rather, proteins and fats are complex structures, immense in size and composition to the simple glucose molecule. Quite possibly the human body under the divine guidance of innate intelligence may not pull into the body (via the cell wall membrane) molecules of such size. Instead in observance of the laws of conservation of energy, the body will "take in" these macronutrients on an "as needed basis". Why expend the energy for something that isn't needed? The six carbon glucose molecule however, being as small as it is, simply enters via the gut and spikes the blood glucose level. The liver, pancreas (and possibly the adrenals) then have to respond to this assault on a reactionary basis with a corresponding "roller coaster" of hormonal, physiological and emotional changes.

But eating fats and proteins will increase my cholesterol and trigyclerides!

The mainstream population has been erroneously led to believe that eating carbohydrates is healthier and more intelligent than fats and proteins. Medical science appears to differ in this belief however. It is factually stated in the medical texts that eating excess carbohydrates forces the liver to convert them into trigylcerides and cholesterol.

A woeful tale of triglycerides and cholesterol!

"When glucose is not immediately required for energy, the extra glucose that continually enters the cells either is stored as glycogen or is converted into fat. When the cells approach saturation with glycogen, the additional glucose is the converted into fat in the liver and in fat cells and then is stored in the fat cells."[6]

Guyton's Textbook states quite clearly, "Whenever a greater quantity of carbohydrates enters the body than can be used immediately for energy or stored in the form of glycogen, the excess is rapidly converted into triglycerides and then stored in this form in the adipose tissue."[7]

Further, "Besides the cholesterol absorbed each day from the gastrointestinal tract, which is called *exogenous cholesterol*, an even greater quantity is also formed in the cells of the body, called, *endogenous cholesterol*. Essentially all the endogenous cholesterol that circulates in the lipoproteins on the plasma is formed by the liver, but all the other cells of the body form at least some cholesterol, which is consistent with the fact that many of the membranous structures of all cells are partially composed of this substance."[8]

The plasma cholesterol concentration is more correctly influenced (or directly attributed to) by the consumption of carbohydrates and their conversion to fats as a "survival/adaptation" mechanism of the body. Concomitantly the plasma cholesterol levels are controlled by a feedback mechanism and can actually be controlled/stabilized by ingestion of fats.

It's not the fats...
it's the carbohydrates stupid...

Thus, eating external sourced dietary fats (exogenous) really does not increase the internal fat levels (endogenous). In other words eating carbohydrates raises the cholesterol level more than eating the fats. The fats actually have a dampening effect on the livers own internal production.

This again is clearly illustrated in Guyton's, "An increase in the amount of cholesterol ingested each day increases the plasma concentration slightly. However, when cholesterol is ingested, the rising concentration of cholesterol inhibits one of the essential enzymes for endogenous synthesis of cholesterol, thus providing an intrinsic feedback control system to regulate plasma cholesterol concentration. As a result, plasma cholesterol concentration *usually* is not changed upward or downward more than ± 15 percent by altering the amount of cholesterol in the diet."[9] Guyton continues by adding that "Ingestion of fat containing highly unsaturated fatty acids usually depresses the blood cholesterol concentration a slight to moderate amount."[10] And finally, "The blood cholesterol also rises greatly in diabetes mellitus."[11]

In a nutshell

Therefore it has been shown that increased ingestion of carbohydrates (both simple or complex) does more to increase the blood levels of cholesterol than eating proteins and fats, both of which are major constituents of the human body. Regarding proteins and fats, the body takes what it needs from outside sources while compensating for its deficiencies and excesses with internal controls.

No part of the human body is made up of carbohydrate or glucose. Carbohydrates whether complex (ie: potatoes, rice) or simple (ie: candy bars, cupcakes) are simply broken down into a simple six carbon atom molecule called glucose. Glucose is a poison to the nervous system and being as small as it is (six carbon atoms) readily enters the blood stream. It destroys nerve tissue throughout the body such as sensory/motor nerve, eye retinas and the brain! The body in keeping with the homeostatic will to survive, converts this glucose into a substance that is safer and of which the body (the nerves, brain and all the cell membranes) is actually made from – cholesterol.

The ingestion of fats and proteins is shown to suppress the internal production of cholesterol. This is quite possibly the most natural form of "statin control" possible. The body again in keeping with homeostatic control will always attempt to conserve energy. This is the biological law of conservation of energy. The human body with proper communication between the higher brain centers and tissue levels (ie: intact functioning nervous system) will not waste energy pulling into itself macromolecules as large as long chain fatty acids and large protein molecules that it doesn't readily need. These compounds while inside the "gut" are still "outside" the body. The human body is composed of such molecules and can synthesize these on an as needed basis from internally stored reserves and externally provided diet.

A True Food Pyramid

Following the adage of "Eat what you are!" a more logical construct for a typical food pyramid would be to examine what the human body is composed of. Water being the major compound of the body would be the largest component, followed by protein, fats and lipids, vitamins / minerals and other micronutrient rich foods. The smallest portion of this food pyramid is carbohydrates.

Water, the Matrix of Energy

The physiological importance of water for true optimal health has been extolled in the numerous writings of Dr. Batmanghelidj, MD. The water we ingest should be the purest possible and with the energetic vitality left intact or reintroduced. Generally two thirds of an ounce of water per pound of body weight is considered the ideal water formula. This equates to roughly one quart per fifty pounds of body weight. Naturally under more extreme climates this may need to be altered. Additionally to prevent any possibility of a hyponatremic (low sodium) condition, the proper addition of a healthy source of sodium such as vegetable (celery) or high quality sea salt would be advised.

Water not only provides its chemical value to the body but can and does impart its "energetic signature." Various energetic frequencies have been shown to be carried via the medium of water in such applications as homeopathy. It must also be noted that negative energies from improperly processed water can also be transported to the human body upon ingestion. The works of Masaru Emoto, MJ Pangman, Mu Shik John, Jana Shiloh and many others have clearly identified the existence of this phenomenon.

Protein, the Building Block of Life

The most logical source of protein is from a high quality animal source. Animal based protein includes all the essential amino acids needed by the body. This may seem startling to some but it is not only the most intelligent but logical choice. The body does not need to break down (catabolize) animal protein to each individual amino acid in order to rebuild its cells, thus conserving energy. Plant based proteins need to be catabolized further and then rebuilt back to human tissue. This is a much more inferior process, especially when the body may not be communicating properly between the higher brain centers and the tissue levels.

Dr. Don Colbert, MD says it best in his excellent book, *Dr. Colbert's "I Can Do This" Diet* "Animal proteins are typically a higher-quality protein than plant proteins and contain all the essential amino acids. This category includes dairy, eggs, meat poultry and fish, all of which have all the essential amino acids needed and thus are a higher-quality protein." [12]

To Grill or Not to Grill

It is interesting to note that the first human ancestor to use fire to cook food was *homo erectus,* somewhere between 1.8 million and 800,000 years ago. [13] This resulted in notable anatomical changes such as smaller teeth and jaws facilitating the beginnings of speech. More remarkable is the tremendous increase in size of the cranial vault for housing a larger brain! [14] Thus cooking over fire (grilling) promoted an evolutionary shift in the development of mankind by allowing speech communication and increased brain developmental skills. The world's foremost authority, ambassador and author on live-fire cooking, Steven Raichlen reports, "In his fascinating book, *Catching Fire: How Cooking Made Us Human,* Richard Wrangham points out how much easier a diet of cooked food is to chew than the raw foods eaten by other primates then and now." [15] It is indisputable that cooking and heat causes this denaturing of the long chain protein molecule, allowing an easier and more efficient digestive process. Simply observe the morning after aromas of putrefying raw meat wrappers in the trash can!

Fats and Lipids the Great Communicators

Much has been written about fats and lipids. Obviously a diet rich in animal based proteins will also provide many of these much needed nutrients. World renowned nutrition expert Nora T. Gedgaudas, CNS, CNT adds, "Most organs and tissues in the body, including the brain, actually prefer, if we let them, to use *ketones,* the energy-producing by-products from the metabolism of fats. There is abundant evidence that many modern disease processes, including those resulting in cardiovascular disease, elevated triglyceride levels, obesity, hypertension, diabetes, hypoglycemia, and cancer, to name a few, are the product *not* of excess natural fat in the diet, but of excess carbohydrates." [16] Once again it's not the fats that elevate, it's the carbohydrates! Multiple studies ranging from Framingham, the Minnesota State Hospital Trial, the Veterans Clinical Trial, the Puerto Rico Heart Health Study and the Honolulu Heart Program have all shown a consistent, distinct lack of correlation between dietary fat, dietary or serum cholesterol, and heart disease. [17]

The Micronutrients

It is undeniable that the human body requires a rich source of natural vitamins, minerals, probiotics and other food/soil based micronutrients. These should be obtained from whole food organic, non-irradiated and non-genetically engineered sources. Plant based sources as well as animal sources will inherently provide vitamins, minerals, fibers and many other micronutrients. Naturally it is only logical to consume vegetables and fruits in as fresh a state as possible. It is here that the heat sensitive nutrients are provided in their raw state.

Cooking may release the availability of certain vitamins but can destroy certain enzymes and cofactors. Do not confuse this with cooking of the animal proteins mentioned earlier. Cooking the protein makes the amino acids and short chain proteins more available,

and that is the purpose of eating such proteins. Although many highly important vitamins/minerals are obtained from animal sourced meat, poultry and fish, the reason for eating these cooked, differs from the reason for eating plant sourced food stuffs raw.

And Finally... the Carbs!

World recognized, esteemed author and nutrition researcher Nora T. Gedgaudas states it best, "Carbohydrates, other than the largely indigestible variety found in fibrous vegetables and greens, have generally played a minimal role at best through most of human evolution. In fact, of all the macronutrients (that is, protein, fats and carbohydrates), the only ones for which there are no actual human dietary requirements are carbohydrates. This is a critical and very fundamental point to remember: **we don't ever have to eat any sugar or starch of any kind at all in order to be optimally healthy.**"[18] The most logical source for the carbohydrate component would be a natural, unprocessed, complex food source.

The Energetics of Life

Steve Gagne in his monumental work, *Food Energetics: The Spiritual, Emotional, and Nutritional Power of What We Eat*, explains the entire realm of energetics as it pertains to the food choices and methods of preparation of these foods. He states, "Ancient peoples, through their relationships with the plants and animals providing their food, understood that their food conveyed the unique energetic qualities of its source, such as swiftness from wild deer and groundedness from root vegetables."[19] Food is not only composed of macro and micronutrients but also conveys the subtle rhythms, harmony and energies that are so important to the expression of optimal health. This concept is absolutely the most astounding evidence to support the health building qualities of eating properly.

Gedgaudas sums it up best when stating, "So many taboos... have likely risen from the perception of 'you are what you eat.' Consider instead, that *you are what your metabolism does with what you eat.*"[20] So if you eat vegetables... you're a veggie, if you eat fruit... you're a fruit, if you eat meat.... well, you are meat. Therefore...

Eat What You Are!™

Dr. Hyman's Food Pyramid

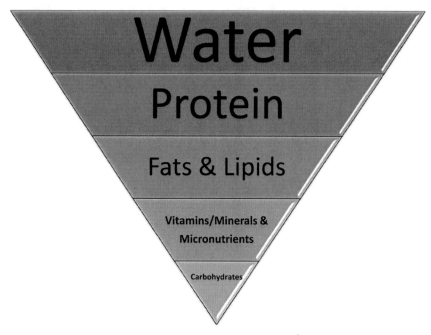

1. Arthur C. Guyton, MD, *Textbook of Medical Physiology,* 7th ed. 2 (Philadelphia: W.B Saunders, 1986), 841.
2. Ibid., 861.
3. Ibid., 837.
4. Lubert Stryer, *Biochemistry,* 2nd Ed. (New York: W.H Freeman, 1981), 385.
5. Ibid., 407.
6. Guyton, 816.
7. Guyton, 822.
8. Guyton, 825.
9. Guyton, 825.
10. Guyton, 825.
11. Guyton, 825.
12. Don Colbert, MD, *Dr. Colbert's "I Can Do This" Diet,* (Lake Mary, Florida: Siloam, 2010), 76.
13. Steven Raichlen, *Steven Raichlen's Planet Barbecue!,* (New York:Workman Publishing, 2010), XI.
14. Ibid., XI.
15. Ibid., XI.
16. Nora T. Gedgaudas, CNS, CNT, *Primal Body, Primal Mind: Beyond the Paleo Diet for Total Health and a Longer Life,* (Rochester Vermont: Healing Arts Press, 2011), 10.
17. Ibid., 12.
18. Ibid., 9.
19. Steve Gagne, *Food Energetics: The Spiritual, Emotional, and Nutritional Power of What We Eat, (Rochester, Vermont: Healing Arts Press, 2008),* back cover.
20. Gedgaudas, 70.

APPENDIX B

RECOMMENDED RESOURCES

The following are some recommended resources for obtaining products and information mentioned throughout this book.

Websites

www.wellnesslecture.com

It is a delight to become informed and send others for the same. Use fred@ewater.com as the referring email to log in and view or listen to the Adrenal Exhaustion lectures. There are many excellent lectures available on this site, with more being added regularly.

www.ewater.com/fred

Products available here include water filtration appliances, including shower filters, whole house systems, and reverse osmosis systems. The Vitalizer Plus™, Quantum E Crystals, EP2 Pendants, eMugs, Cell Bugs, and many other EMF protection devices are also available. Air purification and virtually all foundational health support products are found on this site. A true one stop shop of uncompromised quality.

www.trinisol.com

This site is the ultimate source for fermented nourishment and foundational support for the body. Here you will find the "Bulldozer" pack including Synbiofood™, Super Critical EFA's™, Biotical™, Quanta Water™, Perfect Balance™, MuscadineMax and the EP2 Stress Pendant.

www.naturalsolutionsfoundation.org
Natural Solutions Foundation, Dr. Rima Laibow, MD, Medical Director, remains the most accurate source of information on vaccinations, health legislation and other health related information. It is a superb resource, worthy of our support, financially and otherwise.

www.healthfreedomusa.org/
This is another Natural Solutions foundation website for those who wish to take proactive steps to "push back" against the encroachment of our health freedoms.

http://energywater.com/
This site helps add clarity to energy water catalysts, technologies and bottled waters now available.

www.fredvanliew.com
Fred Van Liew's personal blog and referenced articles on Politics affecting Health, Water, Air & Energy.

www.wellnessclubsofamerica.com
Dr. Dale Peterson, MD, offers years of wisdom and practical solutions to health challenges. A family practitioner, lecturer with appearances on international Christian and secular radio and television, he has provided us all with a must have resource web site. It is a gold mine of information.

www.ktradionetwork.com
Kevin Trudeau has done more to educate the masses on natural health support and cures, in understandable language, than any person in history. His books have sold over fifty million copies, and his radio broadcasts contain uncensored truths.

www.hthradio.net
Hosting Fred Van Liew's "Your Health, Your Choice" radio broadcasts and archived programs, Highway to Health radio

allows Fred to be his usual non politically correct self, putting out the truth as he finds it on health, including both the politics and the solutions.

www.intacthealth.com
This site contains Dr. Leonard Coldwell's Instinct Based Medicine Store products, including books, tapes, product specials and more. Stress and emotions cause nearly all disease. Find out how to include the remedy for stress from the world's best. His *The Only Answer to Cancer* is a must read!

www.mercola.com
Without question this site deserves its reputation as one of the most reliable sources of health information on the web. Always well researched and well communicated. Comprehensive.

Recommended Books
Carlo, George and Schram, Martin. *Cell Phones: Invisible Hazards in the Wireless Age.*
Coldwell, Leonard. *Instinct Based Medicine.*
Coldwell, Leonard. *The Only Answer to Cancer.*
Jhon, Mu Shik. *The Water Puzzle & The Hexagonal Key.*
Miller, Neil Z. *Vaccine Safety Manual.*
Morter, M.T. *Correlative Urinalysis.*
Pangman, M.S., M.J. *Hexagonal Water: The Ultimate Solution.*
Smith, Jeffery M. *Genetic Roulette: The Documented Health Risks of Genetically Engineered Foods.*
Smith, Jeffery M. *Seeds of Deception.*
Yiamouyiannis, John. *Flouride: The Aging Factor.*

Recommended Doctors
Dr. Robin C. Hyman, DC, LCP
2727 LBJ Freeway, #410
Dallas, Texas 75234
214-420-5555

Alan Blum, DC
San Diego, CA
619-688-2090

Recommended Healing Methodologies
Total Body Modificaton (TBM)
Neuro Emotional Technique (NET)
Body Specific Analysis (BSA)
Callahan Tapping Technique
God's incredible Promises as found in Scripture.

Supplement Companies
Standard Process®
Used minimally as recommended by the company, these are very good organic whole food based supplements.
Trinisol™
Foundational health support in fermented predigested form. Home of the Health Builder "Bulldozer" Packs.

To Personally Contact Fred Van Liew
1-800-964-4303 Corporate offices
1-800-288-1218 Personal direct
Fred's personal web site: www.fredvanliew.com
email: fred@ewater.com

In most cases Fred still answers his own phone. Most people are so intimidated they don't call, so he is not yet overrun by calls. He will answer all of your questions. Fred asks for just one courtesy – If you're not going to accept his answer, please don't keep asking the same question. He is only going to give you the same answer. It's the only thing that truly aggravates him, because he most likely has one or two calls waiting on the line. He will give you whatever time you need, so long as you don't repeat the same question. Make sure you have gone to www.wellnesslecture.com before you call!

BIBLIOGRAPHY

Bryson, Christopher. *The Flouride Deception*. New York: Seven Stories Press, 2004.

Carlo, George and Schram, Martin. *Cell Phones: Invisible Hazards in the Wireless Age*. New York: First Carroll & Graf Publishers, Inc, 2001.

Coldwell, Leonard. *Instinct Based Medicine*. New York: Strategic Book Publishing, 2008.

Coldwell, Leonard. *The Only Answer to Cancer*. Springfield: Healing Nature Press, 2009.

Cournoyer, Cynthia. *What About Immunizations?* Santa Cruz: Nelson's Books, 1995.

Fisher, Barbara Loe. *The Consumer's Guide to Childhood Vaccines*. Vienna: National Vaccine Information Center, 1997.

Gagne, Steve. *Food Energetics: The Spiritual, Emotional, and Nutritional Power of What We Eat*. Rochester: Healing Arts Press, 2008.

Gould, Jay M. and Goldman, Benjamin A. *Deadly Deceit: Low-Level Radiation High-Level Cover-Up*. New York: Four Walls Eight Windows, 1991.

Hyman, Robin C. *Applied Kinesiology & Subluxation Analysis*. Dallas: Enchantment Publishing, 2009.

Hyman, Robin C. *Table Assisted Adjusting: An Exposition of the Thompson Technique.* Dallas: Enchantment Publishing, 2003.

Jhon, Mu Shik. *The Water Puzzle & The Hexagonal Key.* Coalville: Uplifting Press, Inc., 2004.

Levitt, B. Blake, ed. *Cell Towers: Wireless Convenience? or Environmental Hazard?* Markham: New Century Publishing, 2001.

Levitt, B. Blake. *Electromagnetic Fields: A Consumer's Guide to the Issues and How To Protect Ourselves.* Lincoln: iUniverse, 2007.

Miller, Neil Z. *Vaccine Safety Manual.* Santa Fe: New Atlantean Press, 2008.

Morter, M.T. *Correlative Urinalysis.* Rodgers: BEST Research, Inc., 1987.

Pangman, M.S., M.J. *Hexagonal Water: The Ultimate Solution.* Coalville: Uplifting Press, Inc., 2007.

Smith, Jeffery M. *Genetic Roulette: The Documented Health Risks of Genetically Engineered Foods.* White River Junction: Chelsea Green Publishing, 2007.

Smith, Jeffery M. *Seeds of Deception.* White River Junction: Chelsea Green Publishing, 2003.

Stewart, John Cary. *Drinking Water Hazards.* Hiram: Envirographics, 1990.

Yiamouyiannis, John. *Flouride: The Aging Factor.* Delaware: Health Action Press, 1993.

HEALING SCRIPTURES

Eleven of my favorite healing scriptures.
Word emphasis added by author.

YOU HAVE BEEN GIVEN ALL AUTHORITY OVER THE DEVIL:

Luke 10:19 Behold, I give unto you power to tread on serpents and scorpions, and over all the power of the enemy; and nothing shall by any means hurt you. Notwithstanding in this rejoice not, that the spirits are subject unto you; but rather rejoice, because your names are written in heaven.

IT IS YOUR SPOKEN WORDS AND ACTIONS THAT ALLOW THE HAND OF GOD TO MOVE:

John 14:12-14 Verily, Verily I say unto you, He that believeth on me, the works that I do shall he do also; and greater works than these shall he do also; because I go unto my Father. And whatsoever ye shall ask in my name, that will I do, that the Father may be glorified in the Son. If ye shall ask anything in my name, I will do it.

PRAYER OF AGREEMENT:

Matthew 18:19 Again I say to you, That if two of you shall agree on earth as touching anything that they shall ask, it SHALL be done for them of my Father which is in heaven. For where two or three are gathered together in my name, there am I in the midst of them.

LACK OF DOUBT:

Mark 11:22-24 And Jesus answering saith unto them, Have faith in God. For verily I say unto you, that whosoever shall say unto this mountain, Be thou removed, and be though cast into the sea; and SHALL NOT DOUBT in his heart, but SHALL believe that those things which he saith SHALL come to pass; he SHALL have whatsoever he saith. Therefore I say unto you, what things soever ye desire, when ye pray, believe that ye receive them, and ye SHALL have them.

NO GRUDGES:

Mark 11:25 And when ye stand praying, forgive, if ye have ought against any: that your Father also which is in heaven may forgive you your trespasses. But if ye do not forgive, neither will your Father which is in heaven forgive your trespasses.

THE SIGNS THAT SHALL FOLLOW EACH OF US THAT TRULY BELIEVE:

Mark 16: 17-18 And these signs SHALL follow them that believe; In my name SHALL they cast out devils; they SHALL speak with new tongues; They SHALL take up serpents; and if they drink any deadly thing, it SHALL not hurt them; they SHALL lay hands on the sick, and they SHALL recover.

CLAIM YOUR HEALING, DON'T ASK FOR IT. IT HAS ALREADY BEEN GIVEN:

1 Peter 2:24 Who his own self bare our sins in his own body on the tree, that we, being dead to sins, should live unto righteousness: BY WHOSE STRIPES YOU WERE HEALED (Isaiah 53:5 "we are healed")

GOD'S ANSWER TO ALL HIS PROMISES IS ALWAYS YES (IF YOU KNOW THEM AND BELIEVE WITHOUT DOUBT):

2 Corinthians 1:20 For all the promises of God in him are yea, and in him Amen, unto the glory of God by us.

READ YOUR SCRIPTURES OUT LOUD DAILY:

Romans 10:17 So then faith cometh by hearing, and hearing by the word of God.

ASK THE HOLY SPIRIT TO GIVE YOU UNDERSTANDING EACH TIME BEFORE YOU READ:

John 14:26 But the Comforter, whom the Father will send in my name, shall teach you all things, and bring all things to your remembrance, whatsoever I have said unto you.

HEALING POWER COMES FROM THE ANOINTING WITH THE HOLY GHOST

Acts 10:38 Now God anointed Jesus of Nazareth with the Holy Ghost and with power: who went about doing good, and healing all that were oppressed by the devil; for God was with him.

Basic Summary: These are the basic steps recommended in this book to follow when recovering from exhausted cell function that has led to adrenal exhaustion or chronic fatigue:

- Acknowledge that modern nutrition does not address the harmonic support needed for cellular support energetically. Providing the body with fermented, predigested support, along with polarized EFA's, is the most efficient solution. Most importantly harmonic coherent energy sources must be included. Avoid stimulatory supplements and liquids.

- Genetically modified foods must be replaced with non GMO plant sources and meats not fed GMO grain.

- Water, whether tap or bottled, today has little structure or coherent energy. Both are needed to provide efficient hydration and cellular support QuantaWater, Perfect Balance or Harmony Drops recommended. VitalizerPlus technology also an option. You must start with purified water.

- Thoughts determine body response to stress. Only through personal responsibility for the words crossing our lips and the thoughts we entertain in our mind will we provide a supportive environment within our bodies. Daily input through reading and audio recordings is essential to reprogramming poor thinking.

- Probiotics and fermentation are the keys to restoring support for the living organisms within the body. These living commensal cell organisms will create the vitamins on demand, while going after minor infections and pathogens. Biotical ferment is an exceptional resource.

- Antioxidant rich foods or natural whole food supplements are essential, particularly in the early weeks of restoration. MuscadineMax is an excellent resource for this purpose.

- Personal protection from environmental chaos of all types is essential. This includes computers, cell phones and cell phone towers, satellite microwaves, radio signals from all sources, negative mental thoughts, electrical interference and negative geopathics. The EP2 Stress Pendant is perhaps the most effective appliance for this purpose.

- Consider a first month "bulldozer" approach to getting inside support for the body. Learn more about this on www.wellnesslecture.com.

- Remember that ultimately, all healing comes from God. What we do is stewardship for the body. Know that no one was given a defective body or organ. Something we have done or are doing has or is causing disfunction or disease.